Break/Through

Healing Obesity, Debt and Depression –
One Chakra at a Time

Katie Custer

First Edition published in 2009.

Front cover art: *Swept/Vivid* Copyright ©2005 Katie Custer
Front cover design and back cover photo: Judy Custer

ISBN-10: 0-615-38257-6
ISBN-13: 978-0-6153825-7-9

Library of Congress Control Number: 2010910218

www.chakra-girl.com

I wrote this book for you.
For you, the survivor.

You know who you are. You are reading this right now.
I wrote this book for that part of you, deep inside, that has
been waiting. Waiting so patiently.

Your time is now.

Let this be the beginning of your own breakthrough.

Table of Contents

Acknowledgments

This book initially flew out of me as a sort-of blurt, topping out at around 300 pages. The moment I finished typing it, all I remember thinking is that *I've said everything that I needed to say.* I thought I was done and set it aside. Weeks later, after hosting a workshop on storytelling (telling your own story), an attendee offered her editing services. The giant blurt subsequently evolved into a manuscript. For many months afterward, working with the manuscript transformed me from a blurter into writer...even into an editor in my own right. Now that its evolution is complete, I have some business to attend to.

First, thank you Laura and Paul, Reiki Master Teachers. You were the first to teach me about energy. Knowing you were both there for support, whether I reached out for it or not, was enough to help me feel safe and believe that choosing to heal would be the right path. An extra moment of gratitude to you, Paul, as you were there to help when I entered crisis - the morning after the memories started surfacing.

Thank you, Tisha, for taking a chance on a first-time author. At the time, I simply wanted someone to listen to my story. You were the perfect midwife for the beginning of this journey.

Thank you to my family for choosing to stick around as I continually remembered, and then documented, difficult details about my past. I was prepared to be left behind and it did not happen. I recognize how blessed I am.

Thank you to friends including those who had to leave, those who "just happened to" arrive, and those who have been there all along. Thank you to coworkers and clients for being willing to read the manuscript…learning more about me than you probably ever wanted to know.

Thank you, Carrie, for being so enthusiastic about my writing style, so honest about how this book might fare in the market, and for your willingness to continue supporting my efforts - even as I realized my writing journey was drifting in another direction. I never expected someone like you to come along. I never even knew to ask for the kind of support you provided. Thank you.

Thank you to my mother. You were there to pick up the pieces when I needed it most…just as I was accepting that, deep inside me, there was a writer in the earliest stages of waking up, that I definitely wanted to become her, and that really needed support. Considering the subject matter you were agreeing to edit, I am forever grateful that you followed through. Thank you for being extraordinary.

Dear reader, thank **you** for reading my story and being open-minded to the details of my healing journey. At the beginning of it all, I discovered that my energy body was patiently holding the key to everything: My whole life's purpose, my dreams, my ability to feel joy, my desire to give love. By writing this book, I hope to pass along knowledge that will help you with the same (and more!), when you are ready for such changes. My intention is to make learning about energy - in yourself and in the Universe – accessible (and intriguing!) to you as you live your life, every day. I am excited to share what I have learned.

And finally, from an entirely separate space, thank you to everyone who reads this book and believes my story. Those two acts – listening and believing – are the most powerful things you can offer a survivor of trauma. Those two things are absolutely, completely transformative. They will turn a survivor into someone with the ability to thrive. Every single time.

Katie Custer
February 17, 2009
Oregon, USA

1

Discovering the Energy Body

For a split second, I thought I dreamt it. Opening my eyes, I realized I was not breathing. I was still in my bed. It was dark and very quiet. Nothing outside me had changed. It only took a moment to acknowledge that it was not a nightmare that woke me up. It was a memory; a moment from my early childhood. Somehow, I knew that little girl was me. The memory came as a flash, taking only a nanosecond to surface. I was much smaller, maybe five- or six-years old. It was a beautiful day. The sun's rays were being filtered through the wispy white curtains in my bedroom. I was sitting in my childhood bed, resting. Next thing I knew he was walking toward me really fast. He was a big person and had his hand out, about to cover my mouth. All of a sudden I was really scared, and I flinched –

Suddenly awake, I was an adult again, laying there in the darkness of my quiet bedroom. Though the moment was over, all of the sensations remained. I still felt five- or six-years old. Though it was thirty years later and the man was long gone, I still felt terror and wanted to hide. I yanked the covers over my head, trying to catch my breath. I felt a sharp pain in my chest as I started to cry. Once the tears came, the pain diminished. After what felt like an hour, I calmed down. It dawned on me that I just experienced something I had heard of before. It was a flashback. In one moment, lasting less than a second, my body released a bit of memory that had been repressed. It had been too traumatic to remember before that moment. This memory was simultaneously disturbing and intriguing.

As it happened, I had not been able to remember much of my childhood before the fifth grade. When I was a teenager I joked that something bad must have happened to me because I could not remember being a kid. That night, in less than a second, I was given the reason why. Though the memory did not specifically show it, my gut confirmed the only thought in my head: I had been abused as a little girl. The rest of that scene was buried so deep that I would not be able to remember more for quite awhile. In that moment, I wanted information, answers to the questions that subsequently rushed into my head.

At the time this memory surfaced, I was in my second year practicing massage therapy. I had also been in training to practice Reiki (pronounced RAY-key), a form of ancient Japanese energy healing. In the West, we call this practice the *laying on of hands*, or *healing touch*. I had just learned how to focus energy to help myself and others heal from trauma, past and present. Focusing energy to help others is the same as focusing it to self-heal. I was still in training and not quite confident enough to do energy work with my clients. In the meantime, I was practicing it on myself. In most cases, doing self-Reiki will promote relaxation and stress relief. I had been doing it nightly for a few weeks with the intention of increased relaxation and more restful sleep.

That nanosecond of memory became a pivotal moment in my life. It marked a change in direction, personally and professionally. Nearly everything about my life needed an overhaul. For years I tried very hard to achieve such a thing, with negligible results. This childhood memory gave me a glimpse of a much earlier time. Before that moment, I thought I knew who I was and where I came from.

Now I could see that I knew very little. Though I did not know exactly what to do next, one thing was certain: it was not going to be easy. Once I dedicated myself to change, however, it occurred to me that I had a myriad of tools available to help me along the way.

As a massage therapist, I already knew a lot about the behavior of the physical body. Muscles store stress and emotion and those things can be released with massage. The mystery that remained for me was exactly *how* the muscles stored these things and exactly *what* those muscles released to give clients such relief. I had a feeling that energy was the missing link. Even before this memory surfaced I had the intention of finding out how energy functioned in the physical body. When I learned how to heal with energy, my sole intention was to help existing clients find more relief. That flash of memory was a sign, however, that I could only see the tip of the iceberg. I was about to learn the truth about my life. Everything changed when I learned about energy.

Energy flows through all living creatures, as well as the earth. In this book, I address the energy that flows through us, individually. The energy that runs through your body is unique to your development, your own life experience. Everything that affects you emotionally and physically also affects you energetically. Your emotions, behaviors, and physical health are strongly affected by the energy that flows through your physical body. This energy, which I call your energy body, has a particular structure, or anatomy, which constantly interacts with and influences your physical anatomy. By understanding how your energy flows, you will become more aware of how your emotions and behaviors have contributed to your physical health and, ultimately, have created the life you are currently living.

Learning about your energy body will help you make permanent changes in your emotional, behavioral, and physical health. Some of these changes will be swift, while others may take more time. Healthy, permanent change is absolutely possible. Reiki is one way to affect such change. Reiki can reveal where energy imbalances exist, guide you to the source of those imbalances and help you understand how to heal them, subsequently restoring balance to your overall health. Once balance is restored, you are more likely to think clearly, be open to inspiration, and to feel a sense of calm where there was once only irritation, restlessness, or anxiety.

I regularly remind my clients that they are the experts on their own bodies, which often comes as a shock to them. While I am not suggesting that they leave Western medicine behind, I am asking them to consider paying more attention to what their body is telling them. One way to listen is by becoming more familiar with the energy that flows through the human body. A few years ago, it occurred to me that the energy body may hold all the answers to complete healing, emotionally and physically. Every day, I am reminded that my own life is proof of this theory.

Some clients come to me through a chiropractic clinic. They present cases of whiplash, low-back and hip pain, usually as a result of recent automobile accidents. Their pain came from recent injury. For some time, I thought the symptoms these individuals reported were completely different from what my private clients were dealing with. While my own clients had neck, shoulder, and low back pain, it was long-term and some of them even called it *chronic* because they could not seem to get rid of it. One day it occurred to me to listen more closely when each of them, at the clinic and in private practice, talked through a session. I already had the sense that talking, just like laughing or crying, was a way to release energy. This time, I had the feeling I should pursue that thought and listen more closely. I was about to find out much more about them than they originally shared. Starting with the very next client, obvious patterns started emerging.

In a session with the first client, working on the muscles of his lower back, he briefly shared how stressful his job was. He then elaborated about insecurities in his relationship and home life. The only time he paused was when I moved onto the next set of sore muscles. His shoulders and neck were tight and, when I began massaging them, the topic shifted. He talked about being too shy to speak up in an important debate at work. When I returned to his lower back he paused and then revisited issues surrounding his relationship and home life. It became clear that his emotional stress was directly affecting his physical body, with each stressor taking up residence in a specific area. While I knew the physical body somehow stored emotional stress, I did not realize how intricately designed this storage facility was.

After a few sessions, this client was feeling relief and asked me what has become a common question. Is there is a way to get rid of recurring pain once and for all? I told him I believe that massage and other forms of bodywork can only guide him to the cliff's edge, on the way to whole health - but how he lives his life is the key that will ultimately deliver more permanent healing. In the end, we must all choose to be active in our healing process. By learning about the energy body and its imbalances we will be able to identify attitudes, choices, and behaviors that are counterproductive in our pursuit of overall wellness.

My understanding of energy and how it related to human anatomy evolved with each client. Each presented examples of how emotions were being stored in their muscle fibers and that those emotions were building up enough to cause, or intensify, physical pain. These clients presented specific examples relating directly to the energy body and its structure, the Chakra System, which I had learned about in Reiki training. The Chakra System is the organizational structure, or the anatomy, of the energy body. Each Chakrum is a central location of energy flow. The energy body is composed of seven main Chakras, or locations where energy gathers and then travels outward, through the body. Each Chakrum relates, specifically, to a different region of the physical body. Energy flows into each Chakrum, then out and into the next Chakrum. If something causes this energy to slow down or stagnate, such as a traumatic incident or interaction, it creates an imbalance in this energy flow.

11

Think back to a moment when something shocked you, causing you to suddenly hold your breath. The shock created a moment of pause in your body's energy flow. If the shock was not immediately resolved and calm restored, your energy body was affected. Before the shock, your energy was balanced and flowed as steady as a regular drumbeat. The moment you were shocked, the drumbeat changed. When the shock is resolved and peace is restored, the drumbeat is either able to return to its previous, soothing pattern or at least establish a new, consistent beat. If there is no resolution, however, and calm is not restored, a different, more erratic drumbeat takes over.

The energy moving through us is meant to flow in a steady, balanced manner. When it becomes imbalanced, the energy body sends signals to let us know something is off kilter. The first warning signs come through intuition, the gut feeling. The second round of warnings comes through how we respond, emotionally, to life experience. Over time, I noticed each client presented a unique example of how energy imbalances impacted their lives. I was bearing witness to an absolute pattern. This pattern was supported by what I had learned in Reiki training and research. Each of the seven Chakras was unique in its location related to the physical body. Each Chakrum was also unique in how its imbalances manifested emotionally, behaviorally, and physically.

While each client presented a unique scenario because of their life experience, the emotions and behaviors resulting from their energy imbalances were strikingly similar to other clients. With this in mind, it became clear to me that specific emotions were related to energy imbalances in specific Chakras. Feelings of insecurity, for example, were expressed by certain clients and related directly to physical pain they were feeling in the location of a particular Chakrum, the Root Chakrum (hips, legs, and feet). Feelings of shame and embarrassment, on the other hand, manifested in a separate physical location, related to a different Chakrum, the Sacral Chakrum (low back, pelvis).

Each Chakrum is unique in how imbalances manifest. Each is also unique in the emotions felt when one's energy is healthy, balanced, and vibrant. A healthy Throat Chakrum, for instance, uses its energy to support self-expression and communication. Neck pain is related to the Throat Chakrum in the energy body. While one person's neck soreness will be about their job, the next person's neck soreness will relate to their partner. In both cases the issue is the same. Clients who report neck pain may feel too shy to speak up at their job or with

13

their partner, have problems communicating when they do express themselves, or feel that their message is being disrespected or ignored which makes them feel silenced. When healthy energy flow in the Throat Chakrum is interrupted regularly because of shyness, being disrespected, or being silenced, it builds up and eventually causes physical soreness. The Chakra System is explored more thoroughly in Chapter 2.

Learning about energy and then seeing how it consistently manifested in my clients, emotionally and physically, was exciting. It felt like I had been let in on a big secret. I knew I could work with energy in order to help my clients release pain and restore health and wellness. At the same time, I was seeing how imbalanced energy manifested in emotions and behaviors in my own life. These discoveries ran parallel, feeding off of each other on a regular basis. It dawned on me that, in addition to helping individual clients learn about their energy body and its health ramifications, I could help guide more individuals toward healing by expanding my reach.

This book developed as my past and present synthesized. Most of my life I did not feel at all like *me*, at least not the *me* I wanted to be. Finding massage therapy was the first step, and Reiki was my second. Massage gave me a vocational *aspiration*, while Reiki became *inspiration* for changing the way I lived my life. In Buddhist thought, the student arrives when the teacher is ready. Originally I pursued Reiki training to help my massage clients on a more profound scale. It was only natural, then, that as a teacher of healing for others I would experience my own transformation. Before long I became a student of self-healing in an equally profound way. For me, self-healing started in a familiar place: body-image and a lifelong struggle with weight. This time, however, instead of focusing on food, which was a symptom, I found myself face to face with the truth.

I have been in recovery for more than three years. I am not an alcoholic or drug addict. My vice is food. For twenty years, I gained weight, lost weight, and gained again. While I attributed this to an inability to control myself around food, deep down I had a feeling that there was more to it. Obesity does not run in my family, so for me, it was behavioral. When I was 31 years old, I discovered what my obesity was covering up. I learned that my deeper issue was repressed memories of childhood sexual abuse. All memories of such abuse had been locked away until that dark, quiet night, only six months into Reiki training.

My recovery from behavioral obesity was launched the night that memory surfaced. My brain had repressed that moment for nearly thirty years. Some people believe it is normal to forget most of one's childhood. I used to agree. Because of this experience, however, I have changed my mind. The years leading up to that night were spent trying to make changes in my life. While my intentions included finding my life's purpose, learning how to live within my means, and finding relief from the flat, gray cloud of depression, I nearly always felt like a failure. I could not figure out why nothing was working for me. Deep down, I resigned myself to feeling that, for some reason, I did not deserve to have a better life.

In the moments after that memory surfaced, however, I had an epiphany. I did not have to keep living the way I was. I did not have to continue to struggle. I was given a single second of truth from my childhood, proof that there was a deeper issue at work in my life. I realized, for the first time, that I had been set up. I had been set up to seek out unfulfilling jobs; to live outside my means, burying myself in debt; and to regularly find myself in situations that made me feel like a failure. In the weeks and months that followed that memory surfacing, I decided to look more closely at the state of my life and how I ended up there. I saw how hard I had actually been working to maintain a life that lacked inspiration and was full of disappointment and failure. These were only some of the scars of childhood sexual abuse, and, for years, they had wreaked havoc on my life and my self-esteem.

Over the next few years, more memories surfaced. It turned out that I had been the victim of abuse on more than a few occasions during childhood. Each of those incidents had further stunted my emotional development. The pattern of abuse had a profoundly negative effect on my self-perception, attitude, and behavior well into adulthood. With every trauma the drumbeat in my energy body grew more erratic, more imbalanced.

As more memories surfaced, related emotions also surfaced. My sense of loneliness grew. Seeking support, I went to a sexual assault crisis center. There I was surrounded by women who had survived similar childhood traumas, as well as many who had recently been victimized. For the first time, I felt acknowledged, respected, and accepted. That was a powerful feeling. I was tasting freedom, secure in the knowledge that I was entitled to much more than what had been forced upon me in childhood. I could move out of survival mode and find out how it felt to thrive. Over the past few years, the word recovery has come to mean more than just physical recovery. I have spent these years trying to change the direction of my life while also trying to piece together bits of who I was as a child. Every day presents new challenges. These challenges changed my life in ways I never thought possible; changes in my behaviors, relationships, eating habits, energy, motivation, and professional opportunities.

None of the changes I've made in my life could have been possible had I not begun releasing the negative energies of my past. By allowing the truth to surface and ultimately facing the traumatic memories from my childhood, I learned to release the emotions, self-defeating patterns, and behaviors that kept my energy stagnant, my spirit tired, and my physical body obese, for so long. By learning about my energy I have learned more about who I really am. While this book reflects my own education and experience with the energy body, I have to say that after years of working with clients I have stopped using the word *coincidence* to describe what we have in common. I hope to inspire you to look at your life, as wonderful as it may be, and find ways to enhance it. Your energy body is storing unresolved issues from your past, some of which may be the cause of unhealthy behaviors. By finally letting go of everyone else's energy you will uncover the true you: your most vital, energetic, compassionate self.

My intention in writing this book is to offer you a road map, something to guide you through your own healing journey.

Everything is Connected

Energy is everywhere. It is outside us, in the natural world, in plants and animals. It is what connects us to each other and to everything in the universe. Energy exists in every part of our physical selves and is constantly moving through our tissues. Your energy body is built in stages and layers. It holds memories. It holds your life story. It uses your cells, your muscles, fat, joints, nerves, blood, organs, fascia and everything else in your body to manifest health crises. It does this because there comes a time in the human experience when the energy body is no longer capable of holding or burying negative emotions. Your body was not meant to hold onto and store things that cause emotional pain. *Emotional pain is a tool to initiate healing*. Your energy body is trying to get your attention.

When something hurts us emotionally, we have a choice of how to respond. We can either express our pain or we can hold it in. If we express it by talking, writing, or otherwise releasing it, we are taking steps toward resolution and healing. If we hold it in, we are forcing our energy bodies to store that moment, blocking our once healthy energy flow. Blockages cause imbalances and, soon, our energy bodies are taking on more emotional pain; pain we are not meant to carry. When it becomes too much to handle, it overflows, affecting our behavior. We act out in order to release some of the stress. In the long-term, however, acting out sometimes proves insufficient in balancing the emotional load. If you are not aware that your emotions or behaviors have changed, your energy body will make things even more obvious. Physical soreness and pain will develop in particular muscle groups. *Physical pain is a tool to initiate healing.* Your energy body is still trying to get your attention.

Your energy body holds all of your unfinished business. If there is an unresolved issue from the past, your energy body stores it until you are prepared to confront it, no matter how long that might take. Everything happens for a reason. Every emotion, behavior, and physical dysfunction has a source. This source may not always be evident. Sometimes your behaviors may stem from conditioning and other times they may be rooted in fear, trauma, or simply getting your needs met. Originally you were taught these behaviors. Your parents, guardians, friends, teachers and mentors were all contributors. The hope is that, overall, these individuals acted from a place of unconditional love. If they did, you grew up in a healthy, safe environment and you learned everything from how to share, to how to communicate, to how to show love, and beyond.

It is important to understand that outside forces such as conditioning and unresolved trauma can cause your healthy energy flow to stop, to become blocked. A blockage in energy flow can ultimately cause health problems. Conversely, unblocking energy flow can restore health to affected tissues.

When a parent, guardian, friend, teacher or mentor acts out of fear or the need to control a child's behavior, their actions may traumatize the child. If a child is yelled at, otherwise abused, or neglected, their energy body is affected. When such incidents are not immediately followed by resolution, explanation, and love, the child remains traumatized. I use the word *trauma* to describe the abuse I survived. In my recovery process I have used such vocabulary with the intention of accepting the truth of what was done to me. This has enabled me to experience a profound level of healing.

When I talk about trauma, I am including a wide range of behaviors that are acted out in order to control an individual. If you are a survivor of combat, or abuse or neglect (whether institutional or personal), those who intended to oppress you taught you certain behaviors. These behaviors guaranteed your survival while, at the same time, made you feel incapable of setting yourself free. They taught you how to be dependent on them so that you would contribute to the cycle of abuse.

Thinking about energy can be difficult because you cannot see it. It is intangible, you cannot physically touch it, yet you have felt your energy drained after a long day of work, or revived after a day of rest and play. When you feel good, it means that however imbalanced your energy body is, the energy flowing through you is enabling you to feel positive, motivated and inspired. Imbalances and low energy flow manifest emotionally as feeling bad, angry, upset, tired, or sick, among other things. This is because energy rides on emotion and emotions ride on energy. When energy gets stuck, so do emotions, and vice versa. Emotions flow when energy flows.

In adulthood, you may feel certain muscles clench when you are interacting with particular people, be it your family, boss, teachers, students, friends or coworkers. You may feel aches, soreness and stiffness in your joints when someone says something that upsets you. Perhaps there is someone in your life who simply makes you feel tired. Your emotional response to these people has manifested physically. If you remain in an environment that causes you emotional stress, your energy body will eventually get tired of processing that stress. Instead of releasing negative emotions, it stores them until there is enough energy to deal with them at a later time. Unfortunately, dealing with them later does not always happen, and those negative emotions remain, unresolved, in your energy body.

As time passes, you may begin to feel soreness or stiffness regularly. These physical sensations are created by those continual environmental stressors and unresolved emotional reactions. Eventually, the stress that caused long term soreness in your neck and shoulders may develop into headaches. If the headaches go untreated, the original stressors and emotional reactions may move into your lower back, causing regular pain in that area. How did this happen? *Pain is a tool to initiate healing.* Your energy body is trying to tell you something. The physical pain you are experiencing may be the result of unresolved emotional issues. Your energy body is inviting you to face these issues and resolve them once and for all.

In my experience, any unusual sensation means my body is trying to tell me something important. By unusual I mean anything that makes me aware of a certain part of my body instead of forgetting about it. This includes but is not limited to pain, soreness, tension, cramping, or tightness. When that happens, I try to pay attention. It is a warning sign. If I take care of it when I feel it the first time, it is preventative. If I wait, chances are good that the next sign will be louder, stronger, or more painful.

Once, I was receiving a massage for recurring pains between my shoulder blades. I was relaxed and drifting off to sleep. The moment the massage therapist found the spot that hurt, however, I was yanked back into reality and launched into a story about a clog in my bathroom sink. I told her about the frustration I felt as I struggled to clear the clog. I recalled being under the sink with the wrench and feeling physically uncomfortable. I could not find an angle that was comfortable for my back and neck. At the time, though I knew I did not have the necessary plumbing skills, I was determined to fix the problem myself. In that moment of impatient plumbing, and at the peak of my frustration, I turned slightly and felt that familiar spot near my shoulder blade tweak a bit. My body had warned me. *That pain was a tool to initiate healing.*

Rather than stopping, I took a quick breath, got angry, and worked for another few minutes. The next message came in the form of a shot of pain that stopped me, altogether. In hindsight, I told her, I was lucky that I had not thrown my back out. That might have happened had I not finally listened to my body. Of course, the pain between my shoulder blades, the cause of my frustration, ran much deeper than simply clearing a hair clog in my bathroom sink. The truth was that I did not want to ask for help, with plumbing or with anything else, because doing so made me feel ignorant and stupid. Though it was an irrational thought process, it felt very real to me. This was an important realization in my life. I was at a point in healing my own energy body that required outside help. Without it, I was stuck. In the end, by reaching out I was able to address this emotional imbalance. I was also able to permanently relieve some of the physical pain I had once considered chronic.

In order to keep track of the memories of abuse that occasionally surfaced, as well as what I was learning about energy, I began journaling. Writing on a daily basis helped me to manage the emotional impact of the whole experience - something I had not anticipated. While I was convinced that I had an energy body, my theory was that it was probably left in pieces and barely functional. As I worked on healing myself, however, it occurred to me that it was actually fully intact and had been all my life. Childhood traumas had only forced my energy body to shrink, making room as others shoved their energy on top of my own. My energy body may have been buried for years, but it was not destroyed. The more I journal and the more I study my emotions and behaviors, the better I feel, physically. I am progressively uncovering my energy body and finally allowing myself to stand up, stretch out, and feel free to move in the space I was originally designed to thrive in.

Your energy body may be buried, but the moment you decide to take control of your life and start unloading all the dead weight, it will bounce right back. Long ago, you learned to survive while still getting your needs met. You learned how to behave in order to keep yourself safe. You were taught behaviors that you carried into adulthood. If these behaviors no longer serve your spirit, and now, perhaps, even cause you emotional pain, it is time to learn that you are capable of changing those behaviors. If you are currently in an abusive situation, however, it is best to take baby steps. There are resources at the end of this book to help you find your way back to yourself.

2

Chakra System

In the physical body, energy exists in the structure of the Chakra System. Just as we have a nervous system, muscular system, and skeletal system, we also have an energy system. This energy gathers in specific locations relative to the physical body. These central locations are called Chakras. The word Chakrum (Chakras = plural) is from ancient Sanskrit, meaning "wheel". In the Chakra System, energy spins around in a manner similar to a pinwheel. Whereas a pinwheel is affected by the wind, each Chakrum is affected by energy flowing through the human energy body.

The Chakras are distributed vertically, generally along the spine, where energy gathers and then flows from one center to the next. These centers of energy have branches, called meridians, which enable energy to travel from the main Chakras to locations throughout the body. While energy is generally flowing through all of the

Chakras from the time we are in utero, each Chakrum also goes through its own more active development process. Pinwheels spin more quickly when there is more wind. In that context, each Chakrum spins more quickly when it is actively developing. Active development means each individual Chakrum has its own span of years during which its energy accelerates. This period of more active, spinning energy supports profound emotional, physical, and spiritual growth in the human life cycle.

Just as Western medicine has mapped out much of the nervous system, Eastern medicine has mapped out the Chakra System. Acupuncturists and other energy healers have charted this system to identify the location of the Chakras as well as to illustrate the flow of energy along the meridians. Some Chakras and meridians line up directly with the nervous system. Often, because parts of the nervous system have this direct relationship with the energy body, sometimes tiny sensations are felt when pressure is applied to certain points.

There are locations the size of pinheads all over the body that, when touched and held, release tension by clearing roadblocks in the meridian system. These locations are used by acupuncturists (with needles), massage therapists and others (with fingertips) in order to help clients find physical and, often, emotional relief. Identifying roadblocks and restoring balance to the Chakra System enables the drumbeat of energy to return to its calmer, more balanced rhythm.

In addition to the nervous system, the energy body also affects, and is affected by, the brain. While emotions are created in the brain, they are often stored in the physical body through the Chakra System. When the energy body has imbalances it will alert us, initially, through our instincts, then through our emotions, and later, behaviorally and physically. To understand how the energy body can be imbalanced, we need to first explore the anatomy of the energy body, itself. It is important to understand the structure of the energy body in relation to the physical body, as well as how the energy body develops over time.

There are seven major centers of energy flowing in the human body. Because they are aligned vertically, along the spine, the first Chakras to develop are called the "lower" Chakras. The next few are the "middle" Chakras and the ones that develop later are called "upper" Chakras. They develop one at a time, starting at the lowest. Each Chakrum is named for the location of the physical body that its energy affects. They are also referred to by number.

The first Chakrum, called the Root Chakrum, is located just below the tailbone. The energy flowing through it affects the physical body from the tailbone downward through the legs, and into the feet. The second Chakrum is called Sacral (or Belly) and its energy affects the pelvis, hips, and reproductive organs. The Solar Plexus (3rd) develops after the Sacral and the base of its energy is just below the rib cage. The lineup continues through the Heart (4th), Throat (5th), Third Eye (6th), and Crown (7th) Chakras. As we move upward along the spine, studying each Chakrum, it will become clear how each correlates specifically to the anatomy and physiology of the region where its energy flows.

Development of each Chakrum corresponds to a span of years in human development. The active development of some of the lower Chakras (Root, Sacral) corresponds to a shorter range of years than the higher (Third Eye, Crown) Chakras. For example, while Root Chakrum development begins in utero and may continue for up to four years, the Crown Chakrum begins active development when we are in our 50s or older and may continue for decades. As each Chakrum enters active development, the Chakrum that is decelerating returns to a more gentle energy flow, in balance with the rest of the energy body.

Although seven major energy centers are widely recognized, Reiki practitioners and other energy healers have sensed more than seven Chakras distributed throughout the body. In this book, I focus only on the seven primary Chakrum centers.

Each Chakrum has a particular span of years when it is actively developing, during which time it is more susceptible to sustaining trauma. That said, however, the energy of each Chakrum can also be affected after its major development has slowed. **This means that unresolved emotional traumas from childhood and adolescence will probably manifest later in life.** Unresolved trauma creates imbalanced energy flow. Such imbalances will manifest emotionally, behaviorally, and physically.

Our energy bodies give us a multitude of opportunities for prevention. Intuition is the first form of communication used by the energy body to get our attention. If we are not aware of our gut feelings or do not act on them, the next method the energy body uses is emotion. Emotional responses and reactions are there as signs that healing and change are necessary and possible.

When the Chakras are balanced, they are not fighting and feeding off each other. They are free to function normally. Healthy energy flow allows for new ideas, increased creativity, motivation and inspiration. This energy flow comes in through the Chakrum that hovers directly above our heads. This is the last of the main seven Chakras and, because of its location, is called the Crown. It is through the Crown Chakrum that we are connected to all of the energy in the world around us. There is energy flowing through every human being as well as every plant and animal on earth. When our energy is balanced and flowing, we can connect to all of it on a more profound level.

On the other hand, when energy is blocked, we may feel fired up with negativity – perhaps anger or resentment. If we do nothing to address and resolve these emotions, we will end up using a lot more energy maintaining the negativity than would be used in addressing it. When we choose to live with negativity, we are more likely to respond to challenging events in our lives with anger or resentment. It is as though our energy body is asking us if we are absolutely sure we want to live this way. When these emotions are repeatedly triggered, they change from being emotional reactions to being emotional patterns.

If, over time, we still do nothing to resolve these emotions, they further affect our energy body. Ignored emotions are the cause of many behavioral problems. If the behaviors are not identified and then resolved, the energy body can become overwhelmed and manifest the issue physically.

Some of our behaviors are the result of old energy we have carried with us, like that grudge we refuse to let die. These behaviors each play a particular role in our emotional, mental and physical dysfunctions. Imbalances in the energy body act in much the same way as imbalances in the physical body, similar to joint or muscle injury. For example, you may have an ache in your right knee and start limping, using your left leg to compensate for the weakness. This limping often leads to pain in the left knee and hip because they are being overused. If this happens, you now have an underused, possibly injured right knee and new, painful sensations developing in the left side of your body.

The energy body functions in a similar way. The physical body is directly affected by physical activity, whereas the energy body is affected directly by experiences and personal interactions. Therefore, the personal interactions we have are extremely important. Energy is exchanged when we interact with each other. This exchange affects us on a profound level and happens whether the communication is verbal or nonverbal.

Our emotions play a significant role in the creation or prevention of pain and illness. *Emotional pain is a tool to initiate healing.* When we recognize that some of our emotions are irrational, we have an opportunity to address their origins. Clearing the emotional imbalances in the Chakra System will not make memories of abuse or traumas disappear. Restoring balance will, however, help to calm our anxieties. When we are calm, we are more likely to notice intense fluctuations in our emotions and reactions. Once we are able to identify them, we can work on resolving them. Resolution implies not only emotional and behavioral balance, but also prevention of future physical illness or disease.

When the Chakra System remains imbalanced, the result is a lack of healthy energy flow in some Chakras while others are over-burdened. This is problematic in the long run. When energy is stifled or blocked in one Chakrum, emotions and behaviors related to that Chakrum become stronger, louder, and more aggressive. For example, if I assert myself and do not get the response I want, I may feel frustrated and, raising my voice, repeat myself. If that attempt still does not deliver my desired response, I may become angry.

At this point, it is critical for me to address my own anger. Each time my frustration and anger build, stress grows in my physical body. It is a short trip from stress to illness, so I must honestly study why the original situation led me to anger so quickly. If I do not do this, I will repeat this scenario time and again. Ultimately, unresolved emotions can lead to serious physical ailments.

On the other hand, the energy body yearns for balance and homeostasis in the same way the physical body does. This means that the moment I decide to begin healing, my energy body will respond. When I began to heal my own energy body, stifled energy and emotions began to flow freely again, affecting more than just my Chakra System.

When balance is restored in the energy body, we feel motivated to make change in our lives. Low energy is often replaced by moderate activity. This, in turn, relieves depression and anxiety. The increase in emotional balance that results often leads to more restful sleep and increased energy in the morning. From there, the momentum builds. More healthy energy flow means more vitality.

As I healed more of my energy body, I wondered what would happen next. When my energy was blocked, I could find no way out of my negative emotions and behaviors. Physically, I struggled with my weight but always ended up feeling like a slug. I was barely living, constantly wrestling with a knot of anxiety, stress and depression. After living that way for so long, what would healthy energy do?

3

The 1st Chakrum: Root

The Root Chakrum, the foundation of the energy body, begins developing before we are born and remains in active development through our toddler years and into childhood. Child development research encourages a variety of activities to establish loving contact with babies prior to birth. Parents are urged to sing, tell stories, and talk regularly to the pregnant mother's belly with the intention of connecting with baby. These initial activities, introduced early in Root Chakrum development, become the foundation for developing energies of survival, security, self-preservation, stability, and the will-to-live.

The Root Chakrum completes active development in early- to mid-childhood. If events in your childhood left you feeling insecure or unsafe, these feelings will become part of your energy body as an imbalance in your Root Chakrum. These are cracks in your emotional foundation. Any structure built on such a foundation will be inherently weak. Avoiding the cracks takes an enormous amount of energy. If your Root Chakrum has cracks and is imbalanced, you may feel like you are always dragging just a bit and your attention can never be completely focused on reaching your goals.

Many of us live with a constant worry about security and stability. Often it is hardly noticeable but in reality these concerns drive the decisions we make about how to behave, where to live, what career to pursue, or how to raise our families. These emotions can be a source of regular fatigue for many people who just cannot muster up the energy to do much more with their lives than they are already doing. They are on autopilot. In the context of the energy body, I call this "survival mode". Many people are so used to living this way they do not realize that there is another option. In my life, survival mode was the result of imbalances in multiple Chakras, beginning with the Root. In Chapter 10, I describe what my version of survival mode looked and felt like.

Root Chakrum energy connects us to the energy of the Earth. In the physical body, this energy affects the tailbone and perineum (midway between the genitals and anus), and then continues downward. Soreness and pain at the base of the spine or in the hips, legs or feet are related to imbalances in Root Chakrum energy.

Color is often used by healers to promote balance and energy clearing in the Chakras. The color of Root Chakrum energy is red. Red often indicates pain, inflammation, swelling and other heat related sensations. This does not mean that imbalances in Root energy will always manifest with such specific symptoms. It simply means that when the above sensations are present, Root energy could use some attention. This could look like a cut on your arm that just will not seem to heal but instead remains painful or inflamed. Consider how such a persistent wound usually makes you feel. If something is not healing as expected, does this worry you? This type of reaction is normal and just happens to contain a degree of insecurity – Root Chakrum energy.

When the Root Chakrum is imbalanced it may manifest in ways that feel, look or sound irrational. This can include eating habits that are more about control than nutrition, alienating attitudes toward people who are attempting to connect with you emotionally, or the assumption that no one truly cares what you think or how you feel. Others may judge these behaviors and thoughts as self-centered or self-pitying. The reality is that an energy imbalance is affecting your self-image on a very deep level.

When trauma happens early in life it causes imbalances at the most basic level of the energy body. If those who were supposed to protect you, keep you safe, and provide security for you failed to do so, you learned that it was up to you to protect yourself. You may have used coping mechanisms such as emotional disconnect, eating disorders, or other self-defeating behaviors in order to feel more in control or secure and as a method of self-preservation. Such thoughts, emotions and behaviors all helped you to preserve your own life. They helped you to survive. As an adult, these behaviors may still be affecting your life in a variety of ways.

In Root Chakrum energy the underlying issues creating imbalance are often distrust and insecurity. On a deep emotional level you may not trust your own ability to handle change. Imbalances may manifest in your personal life or in your career. Maybe you feel stuck in your current job but, as years pass, you regularly talk yourself out of finding a better one. Perhaps you fear making a commitment in a relationship, even if the person feels like your soul mate, because it requires taking an emotional risk with unpredictable results. In either case, the possibility of change makes you feel insecure and uncertain about the future.

While these decisions may appear irrational to others, in the context of the energy body, it makes perfect sense that you would avoid change because your decisions come from a rocky foundation. This unstable ground actively seeks security and control. Maintaining the status quo helps you feel more in control and keeps life predictable.

Having to protect yourself from infancy is exhausting, energetically and emotionally. Although you may know, on a cognitive level, that you can protect yourself because you have maintained your own sense of security your whole life, you may still find it difficult to fully trust. This difficulty is blocking your ability to commit to positive change and emotional growth. All of this happens because your Root Chakrum energy is out of balance.

On the other hand, when the Root Chakrum is balanced, all of those elements find closure and healing. There is a sense of strength and calm on a very deep level. Emotionally, you feel driven and motivated. You feel a sense of vitality and inspiration in all that life brings you. Safety, security and self-trust are inherent.

Behaviorally, healthy Root Chakrum energy manifests as assertiveness and self confidence. Enthusiasm, motivation, and drive are fueled by Root energy. Each day, you wake up knowing that life is proceeding in a manageable way and you can handle any degree of chaos that you experience. Change comes and is welcomed.

What secrets were held in my Root Chakrum?

Though restoring balance to the energy body can start with any of the seven Chakras, I began my own journey at the foundation of the Chakra System. My Root Chakrum was actively developing when I was physically abused the first time. When I was approximately two years old, I had an upset stomach, diarrhea, and was screaming and crying. One of my relatives was taking care of me. I had not yet learned to speak, so my method of communicating was to continue to scream and cry.

While I remember him being angry, losing his temper and physically hurting me to get me to stop, the details that lingered were eye contact, facial expression, and tone of voice. Every time I saw those eyes, that face, or heard that voice, even into adulthood, I felt something inside me catch. As a toddler, the immediate effect this abuse had, energetically, was to cause trauma to my developing Root

43

Chakrum. This relative was supposed to be helping maintain a safe and secure world that I could explore. Instead, I felt physically and emotionally threatened by his actions. My developing sense of safety, security, and the will-to-live were all shaken. There was a big crack in the foundation that my energy body was going to have to build upon.

Because I was a sick child expecting to be comforted and was instead frightened, any time I felt sick in the future I did my best to stifle or otherwise minimize my symptoms. When I was feeling sick it did not matter if one of my parents was in charge or I had a babysitter – either way I feared their reaction to my illness. It was not my fault that I had been in pain and was screaming. This moment of betrayal of love and trust, coupled with future incidents of abuse, evolved into the sense that I was not worthy of love.

When trauma is sustained at an early age, emotions often freeze at that moment in development. If they remain unresolved, they will be repeatedly played out in the future, often well into adulthood. Every time health problems arose, I felt and acted the same way as when I was two years old. I felt insecure, ashamed of being ill and afraid I would be judged when I asked for help.

When I began writing this book, the earliest bits of memory that surfaced were details of an incident when I was three. As with every other surfacing memory, the only proof I have that it happened comes physiologically – in how my physical body reacts in the moments, weeks, and months following the revelation. Within a day of this memory surfacing, I felt sudden soreness in my tailbone, tightness in my upper thigh muscles, and was surprised by the onset of an upset stomach and digestive bug that cleaned out my system over the course of two days. My physical body finally had the chance to release tension that my energy body had been holding since this event first happened.

The next time I was abused was when I was about three years old. My family had taken a road trip to a relative's house, where extended family had gathered for a reunion. In that environment, I was safe and free to play and have fun. Moments after we arrived I was running around, giggling. A second later I was pulled aside by an older relative, hidden from view of the rest of the gathering. He had a frightening expression on his face and a knife in his hand. I felt terror much stronger than any fear I have felt since.

Emotionally, this terror instantly added cracks to the foundation that my Root Chakrum was still actively establishing. Gesturing with the knife, he threatened my life and the lives of my immediate family members. I knew he would kill me if I told them or anyone else what he was doing. What I recall is that I could hear family activities happening nearby while I was hidden from view. I was stuck. He orally raped me. My sense of security, safety and self preservation were all shattered.

When he let me go I walked slowly back to my mother and attempted to find comfort without letting on that anything had happened. I wanted only one thing; I wanted to hide. When I arrived at her side, she did not look at me. She was laughing and having a great time. I needed to hide and so I shifted to get closer to her. She put an arm around me patted my back and told me to go play.

All I wanted to do was find safety. If I had been able to ask for it, she would have readily provided it. She was unaware of what had just happened to me, however, and I could not tell her. In shock, I was only able to stand there making physical attempts to receive shelter. At that age, I did not have the ability to provide my own safety and security. At three-years old, I felt dismissed. In those few moments of my life, the development of my Root Chakrum energy had been interrupted again. The incidents at age two and three traumatized my Root Chakrum and my brain instantly repressed the memories. Details of the family reunion surfaced for the first time when I was 31. The memory of being abused at two years old surfaced while I was working on the second draft of this book.

When memories surface it is important to remember that the images and feelings are translated by the energy body of that same age. In my life experience I have noticed that behaviors that made me feel irrational as an adult were irrational because they were my childhood behaviors surfacing. In those instances I was in my 30s but feeling like a three year-old little girl. When issues related to safety, security, stability, and the will-to-live arose, I found myself reacting as a child would. These days I feel it happening relatively quickly and I now have tools to use to work through and heal those emotions.

When I am faced with a new situation at work or meeting new people I feel my energy withdraw as though I am trying to hide behind my mom's leg, as a three year-old would. The more work I do on my energy body, the more I am in touch with how I am feeling and can reassure myself that what is happening is completely normal. Though these feelings still surface occasionally, the difference now is that I am no longer hard on myself when I feel irrational. My self perception has changed. I know now that it is my choice whether I judge myself harshly or choose to take a deep breath and a gentler approach.

What secrets does your Root Chakrum hold?

4

The 2nd Chakrum: Sacral

The second Chakrum to develop is called the Sacral Chakrum. Active development of this Chakrum starts in childhood, around age three, and continues active development until the child is eight or nine. One person's Sacral Chakrum will begin development by age three while another person's might begin at four. Energy flow, as well as the development of the Chakras, has no cut-and-dry boundaries. Regardless of when active development starts, if early trauma is not resolved, your energy body will remain imbalanced as subsequent Chakras are developing.

The second Chakrum is called the Sacral Chakrum because it anatomically corresponds to the Sacrum bone of the pelvis, where the lowest 5 vertebrae of the spine are fused together as one bone. The tailbone is at the base of these 5 vertebrae. The Sacral Chakrum has also been called the Belly Chakrum, referring to the front of the body.

The center of Sacral energy flow is between the pubic bone and the navel. It directly corresponds with the reproductive organs, bladder, kidneys, and large intestine.

As you work with the individual Chakras you may find yourself more aware of certain colors. The energy in the Chakra System contains all the colors of the rainbow. While the color associated with the Root Chakrum was red, the color associated with the Sacral Chakrum is orange.

Emotionally, the Sacral Chakrum houses the energy of your self-image. Self-image is built, in part, by self-judgment and judgment from others. At this early stage in energy development, you begin to sense that your behavior is acceptable (loved) or unacceptable (unloved).

The development of this Chakrum intermingles with the energy of its precursor, the Root Chakrum. This means that your self-image was originally formed, in part, by how safe and secure you felt as a baby and a toddler during Root Chakrum development. Additionally, it was being molded when your personality began developing, when you acted a certain way around others, and it was affected by how they responded to your behavior. How you behave as an adult is often a continuation of patterns learned while your Sacral Chakrum was developing.

Sacral energy is important in the development of self-love. Creativity, increased feelings of security, and the realization that others exist and will respond to your personality and behavior, are all parts of your Self that evolve during this time in your childhood. In later years, the flow of energy through the Heart Chakrum will create an even deeper sense of self-love and love for others. If Sacral energy is stifled, however, the later development of the Heart Chakrum may also be hindered.

Throughout my Reiki training, emphasis was placed on the connection between the Sacral Chakrum and the energies of sexuality and money. Consider the fact that it is common for children to begin noticing their bodies during the age that the Sacral Chakrum is initially developing. Emotional and behavioral development includes spontaneity, innocent desires for play and pleasure, discovery of what makes you happy, and interaction with others without fear of judgment. The energy of sexuality is enhanced as the energy of self-love grows. Sexuality and self-love establish a strong energetic bond during childhood. This bond will emerge more strongly as the Sacral energy winds down and the next Chakrum, the Solar Plexus, picks up speed.

During Sacral energy development, the play, pleasure and self-discovery of sexuality are of the most innocent kind. Boys begin noticing their penises, girls notice they do not have one, and both genders begin asking questions about their genitals. Building on the security of the Root Chakrum energy, the Sacral energy encourages time for growing children to explore and discover their bodies, and how they are different from others. Sensations in the body come alive. A child may discover how different their skin feels in a variety of situations including being naked, wearing clothes, being in the tub, and playing in the dirt. This is a time of fun and self-discovery.

Trauma to the Sacral Chakrum can manifest in a number of ways. While it is not uncommon for imbalances to appear at the time the Chakrum is originally traumatized, it is more likely that emotions and behaviors surface in years after the particular Chakrum has slowed its development. It is common for imbalances in the lower Chakras to manifest emotionally and behaviorally in adolescence and into adulthood. Overtly sexual behavior (which can also imply an imbalance in the Solar Plexus), or sexual denial and shame can both indicate imbalances in Sacral energy.

One of the telltale signs of imbalance in the Sacral Chakrum is an emotional connection to money that feels difficult or impossible to manage. When self-worth is defined, even in small part, by your income or material lifestyle, there is an imbalance in the energy of this Chakrum. When you were a child you may have learned that the more things you had the more loved you were. Perhaps you saw how happy it made your parent(s) when they bought you things. That lesson may have been internalized, translated to mean having money to buy things will bring happiness.

Being only a couple of generations removed from the Great Depression, our culture remains emotionally attached to money. In that era, our country lived in survival mode, working hard and quietly hoping for a better life. A life with more money would mean a life with less worry. The boomerang effect, however, was that subsequent generations have settled into the idea that money provides all of the answers, solves all the problems. This wrong turn has taken us beyond using money to show love. The power we have given our money has nearly obliterated its actual, sole purpose as a commodity – something traded for goods and services. The energy of love, at home and at peace in a strong, balanced Heart Chakrum (actively developing much later), was never meant to mingle with the earliest developmental energies of self-worth and judgment. Energetically, this generational wound can be healed, thus allowing the energy of love to return to its proper home.

Emotionally and behaviorally, imbalances in the Sacral Chakrum will manifest in a variety of ways. For example, strong insecurity may cause you to work hard to control your behavior in the company of others because you worry about what they will think of you. You might also predict future judgment from others and allow those judgments to steer your current behavior. This kind of emotional processing is energy intensive and leads to greater imbalances in the Chakra System. This kind of activity often leads to depression. Strong feelings of despair about the future, based on past or present life experience, are also related to this Chakrum.

You may talk about feeling stuck, unable to change your current circumstances, and regularly yearn for how things used to be. These feelings and thoughts probably do not feel like a trip down memory lane, however. Instead, comparing present circumstances to your selective memory of how things used to be only causes you to remain emotionally stuck in a place that no longer exists. As a result of feeling stuck, the energy flowing in the Sacral Chakrum remains blocked.

Emotional distress or trauma experienced during the development of this Chakrum is likely to manifest physically as pain or illness in related anatomical areas of the body. Any number of problems may surface including digestive dysfunction, impotence, uterine problems, or bladder and/or kidney irritation or disease. Other issues include stiffness in the lower back, tightness in the hip joints, or muscle knots in the gluteal muscles (rear end) which commonly feel like lower back pain. Many physical dysfunctions occurring as a result of blocks in the Sacral energy may also create dysfunctions in the anatomy related to the Root Chakrum. This is due to the overlapping and closely related development of these two Chakras.

Similar relationships exist elsewhere in the energy body and are dynamic in nature. This means that imbalances in Sacral (2nd) energy can affect Third Eye (6th), or imbalances in Solar Plexus (3rd) can affect Root (1st) until resolution and healing occur. At that point, the mingling energies have served their purpose and the energy body can shifts its flow to accommodate the changes.

What secrets were held in my Sacral Chakrum?

My Sacral Chakrum energy imbalances have manifested, for the most part, emotionally and behaviorally, with one specific physical manifestation. At this time in my childhood I was the victim of sexual assaults. While those memories are fragmented, memory of happiness in my childhood remains even more elusive. From stories my parents tell, I was a girl who loved to dance around and giggle…and I know that it is only a matter of time before those memories surface. In the meantime, I have emotional, behavioral, and physical proof of trauma to my energy body from this time in my childhood.

The sexual abuse I sustained happened during the years that this Chakrum was in full development. Physically, my Sacral energy imbalance manifested as belly fat in my teen years. My energy body knew to pad and protect my exposed and injured Chakrum.

During my 20s, I repeatedly attempted to lose weight. Every time I dieted and exercised, I noticed the upper part of my abdominals burning fat and muscle tone emerging. On a dime, my behavior would change. My once religious practice of daily exercise was abandoned.

After a day or two to passed without working out, I gave up. A couple of weeks went by and I dismissed the hiatus, deciding no harm was done. Weight was re-gained through bingeing and, months later I was back with a fat, soft belly and trying again, sensing somewhere deep inside that I was doomed to fail.

My struggle with body fat, exercise, and weight loss was rooted in body image. In my life, body image was rooted in sexuality. As I will further explain in the chapter on Behavioral Obesity, I learned early on to associate being thin with being attractive, being noticed, and then being truly happy. In my 20s, however, I honestly believed I could not lose weight permanently. That meant I was resigned to feeling less than attractive and, as a result, unable to achieve true happiness.

Though my behaviors and thoughts were irrational, the truth was that if I felt attractive, I knew I would act more confident. If I acted more confident, I would attract more attention to myself. If I attracted attention to myself, only one thing would result. During the years of my original Sacral energy development, the years of my childhood, being noticed brought the fear of impending abuse. The concepts of fun, pleasure, exploring sexuality, and being spontaneous, all energies actively developing at that early age, may have never existed for me in the first place.

Spontaneity frightened me on a deep level. Other people's idea of being spontaneous might be calling a friend and going on an unplanned hike or road trip. They might be enjoying a rented movie on a Saturday and suddenly decide to go dancing. In the past, I had been invited to do similar things and always declined. I felt a need for advanced notice and planning.

The only thing I associated with spontaneity was being abused. Each person had decided they were going to interrupt my world and victimize me. For years, I survived a pattern of spontaneous abuse. While that was the reality, prior to remembering I had been abused, all I knew was that I panicked when invited anywhere, whether last minute or to a place I was not familiar with.

Another Sacral energy imbalance that manifested in irrational adult behavior involved money. After high school graduation, I had every intention of getting a college degree and finding a job so I could make a good living. I was raised by upper middle class parents and lived in a beautiful home, so my idea of a good living meant being financially able to afford "nice" things. With those expectations, and living with an imbalanced energy body, I was setting myself up for failure.

I chose to study art in college because it was the only thing I felt real passion for. I knew I was not comfortable selling my own work and realized, as graduation approached, that I would be unable to make a career out of being an artist. From there, instead of seeking out an entry-level corporate job that may have had growth potential, I found a low-paying position at a non-profit arts company. It seemed I was driven to maintain my position on the lowest rung of the ladder. Imbalanced Sacral energy fed the connection I made between my own low self-worth and the low salary I settled for.

Since my idea of a "good living" involved a high salary and I did not value my own life to nearly that degree, I was never going to make enough money to make that "good living" without some regular help. For me, asking for help meant feeling deep shame and embarrassment. Those emotions are both manifestations of Sacral energy imbalances. Asking for help from my parents meant I was going to those whose earnings I dreamed of and admitting that, as their child, I was not capable to achieving it on my own. My Sacral

Chakrum was imbalanced, in need of a relationship to maintain my emotional attachment to money, and yearned for the conversation.

In my 20s I called home on a semi-regular basis. Ashamed and embarrassed, I had to ask for money to help me make it through this bill or that commitment. Those emotions were tied up with losing weight and bingeing to regain it. Every time I realized I needed to ask for money again, I was filled with enough dread that I lost my appetite. After the money came through and my anxiety was assuaged, I would binge at a rapid pace, comforting myself with thoughts of life changing soon so that I would never have to ask for help again. These issues of money desperation and binge eating would chase each other, one taking months to develop into a problem while the other remained quiet. The issues of weight loss and money were acted out, emotionally and behaviorally, with my body and with my parents, for more than a decade.

Asking for help was not just a source of shame when interacting with my parents. I was already afraid of asking for help when I was sick. This developed into being ashamed of needing help at work or from friends. I was always afraid that I would be judged and they would turn me down. Before I reached out, I sped myself through their possible responses. By trying to predict their reaction to me, I was regularly 'future-tripping'.

To some degree this thought process is normal when working outside your comfort zone. You might call it playing devil's advocate. It can be a helpful exercise when you want to consider all sides of an issue. When this is a normal cognitive activity it might take a few hours to work through, after which some time away from it is healthy before the call is made. In my life, the process was based on shame, embarrassment, and irrational fears of judgment. That means that for me, this activity would last days, sometimes weeks. Considering how imbalanced my energy body was already, however, the process remained circular, going around and around inside my head. I could find no resolution. In any given situation, by the time I reached out days had gone by and I had done little more than analyze the possibilities in the meantime.

Remember that energy does not have cut-and-dry boundaries. While trauma affects the Chakrum that is actively developing at the time, it can also affect the energy of the other Chakras. While my Sacral energy was in active development, and sustaining steady trauma, my Solar Plexus Chakrum was also being damaged though it was not going to start its active development for a few more years.

5

The 3rd Chakrum: Solar Plexus

The Solar Plexus is the third Chakrum and it is your power source. The color associated with the Solar Plexus is bright yellow like the sun, lemons, and the brightest flowers budding in spring. It is the most vibrant color in the rainbow. This Chakrum began actively developing during your pre-teen years and continued throughout your adolescence: the time when you were testing boundaries.

This is a critical time for building self-esteem and self-worth. The Solar Plexus is where the energy related to your *ego*, your identity, developed. A healthy ego is a hard thing to come by and is crucial if you are to present your Self to the world with confidence. While Sacral energy introduced the concepts of self- and external judgment, this is the time in life when you first realize that you actually care what others think of you. Later, this attitude may be tempered or rejected altogether, but during the years the Solar Plexus is initially developing this concern is front and center and is often the motivation for your behavior toward others.

You work from your Solar Plexus to make change in your life. You will draw energy from this Chakrum at various times throughout your life, just as you will draw from the other Chakras when it is most appropriate. You will tap into the energy of this Chakrum when you decide to make big changes in your life, to re-invent yourself.

On the physical body, this Chakrum is located approximately two inches above the navel, under the diaphragm. At the back of the body it is located below the rib cage near the kidneys. Organs affected by Solar Plexus energy include those involved in digestion: stomach, small intestine, liver, pancreas and spleen. The nervous system and skin are also affected by the Solar Plexus.

Many of your brightest and most positive emotions are fueled by the Solar Plexus. Optimism, flexibility, self-confidence, humor, joy, understanding, and laughter are all ways the energy body expresses balance in the 3rd Chakrum.

Anger is the emotion that manifests most strongly when there is an imbalance in the Solar Plexus. Of all positive and negative emotions developing during adolescence, anger is often the one that is

64

most noticeable. This is a useful emotion when the energy is channeled in a productive manner. It is destructive when the flow of energy through the Solar Plexus is blocked by trauma and is channeled in another direction.

Behaviorally, imbalances manifest in many ways. You may become overly analytical, fussy, or have less and less tolerance for the behavior of others. You may develop a short fuse, becoming angry more quickly, or begin wielding power too intensely because of a developing need to feel in control. You might develop prejudices, and then work hard to maintain your narrow view of the world.

Physiologically, imbalances often manifest as ulcers, diabetes, anorexia, bulimia, indigestion or insomnia. You may experience panic attacks, headaches, or nervous system disorders. It is possible to develop allergies, arthritis, auto-immune disorders, depression, chronic fatigue, confusion, skin disorders, or feel ongoing tension you call *chronic* as a result of imbalances in the energy of this Chakrum.

During adolescence, the peak years of Solar Plexus development, there are multiple power struggles occurring: those between peers, parent and child, and those between siblings. Most common is the struggle between parents and teenage children.

As teenagers move through hormonal shifts, powerful emotions are also stirred up and can be fueled by developing Solar Plexus energy. This can result in shifts in relationships. Behaviorally, it is common for teenagers to close in emotionally, increasing the level of secrecy in their lives. At this time in development of the energy body, there is a strong need to find one's independence, be accepted as an individual, and simultaneously find approval within one's network of family and friends.

As with all other Chakras, in the years after the Solar Plexus actively develops, traumas to other Chakras will also affect the energy flowing through this Chakrum. Often this manifests as that increased secrecy, which is actually self-protection. Protection and safety are related to the Root Chakrum and are often drawn from during these years to ensure that the Solar Plexus has the opportunity to develop to its fullest potential. During development, one's source of personal power is gaining strength but is also vulnerable to outside influences. Behaviorally, during these years it is natural for one to act out, to test the boundaries of power and then to withdraw in order to regroup and decide how to proceed.

What secrets were held in my Solar Plexus?

I was nearly 11 years old when my family relocated to another state. That move signaled my permanent physical removal from the town where I had sustained most of my sexual abuse. It also signaled the beginning of non-repressed memories. While many parts of moving to a new city, new school, and making new friends frightened me, most of it has remained in the part of my brain that is easily accessible.

From fifth grade through high school, I can remember many details of my life vividly. Perhaps moving away from the location of my trauma enabled me to finally relax and start being myself without worrying about what might happen when I was noticed. This period of my life ran parallel to the beginning of active development of my Solar Plexus Chakrum.

I was a teenager in the late 1980s and early 1990s. Beginning in middle school, my mother enrolled me, annually, in summer art classes. These programs allowed me to feel safe expressing myself, thus enabling me to relax and experiment more with who I was and allow my personality to stretch out a bit. At the same time, I was exposed to a population of older teens who dressed uniquely compared to common trends at the time. This was the time in pop culture when the term 'alternative' entered social vernacular. I felt a need to dress to express myself: to act, look, and be different. It was the perfect time for me to communicate my power in strictly visual manner.

The first vivid memory I have from this age involved moving away from a school with mandatory uniforms and into a school with no such dress code. My mother helped me shop and also helped me sew clothes to supplement my new wardrobe. I remember feeling a burst of creativity. I also remember not being embarrassed when other girls made comments about my clothes and how different they were from current fashion. Years later, one of my teachers told me she saw me as a fashion plate in the making.

Dressing differently worked because I already felt like I stood out. I was the new girl among already formed cliques...and I was taller than all of them. While I attracted attention, this time it was because of something I was proud of – the taste and creativity my mother and I shared in clothes – and that enabled me to feel safe and confident.

While 5th and 6th grade were held in one of the city's elementary schools, we were joined with other elementary classes for middle school, 7th and 8th grade. This was the last stop before high school, where we were blended, once more, with new kids. Behaviorally, I felt the need to express my individuality with every new grade level. At the time I believed I was crafting my appearance to make a statement to everyone that I was not about to blend in, no matter how much they wanted me to. The truth was that I was afraid I was going to be forgotten in the crowd once I reached high school.

To my imbalanced energy body, being lost in a crowd meant being rendered invisible. Invisibility implied that I would be abuse. The common elements among the abuse details I have remembered included being singled out, caught off guard, and hidden – made invisible to anyone nearby who could have helped. In my old community, it seemed I had no choice. In my new world, however, things were different.

Through my 8th grade year I thought more about high school than anything else. It was not excitement. It was dread. Most of my energy was directed to a mixture of fantasies about meeting a boyfriend (his attention could break through my armor and make me feel special) and fears of being stared at by more new kids and judged for the individuality that I displayed. I may have feared judgment but I feared invisibility even more. As the end of the year and 8th grade graduation approached, I thought I knew what would make me feel better about the imminent transition.

The outfit I picked especially for 8th grade graduation was a white cotton dress with a lace collar. It was beautiful, but there was something missing from it. I was missing from it. The day of the ceremony, I was picked up from the salon where my mother was a bit shocked to see that I had the stylist shave the sides and back of my hair close to the scalp. The top was longer and tousled with gel. With the addition of strappy white shoes I called "Jesus sandals", a ring on every finger, and a scowl on my face, I was ready to walk up the aisle of the church with my classmates for the Catholic graduation mass.

Expressing who I was through my hair, clothing, and accessories was an exercise to test my own Solar Plexus energy, and it regularly exhausted me. I was nicknamed "good girl" because I did not act like a belligerent teenager although I spent a great deal of time future-tripping about it. Even if I wanted to act out and break the house rules, I was too tired to try. I had a feeling, much deeper and impossible to decipher, that really, really bad things would happen if I acted out or went out and got in trouble while with friends.

Because of my history of trauma and fear, I was slow to trust others. Friendships were few and I had the feeling that it was safest for me to stay home if I was not at school. Classmates would spend time with each other on weekends at someone's house and I would hear about it the next Monday. I was invited and remember going to one or two gatherings, but I did not feel safe because I did not know the surroundings, so I did not join these groups on a regular basis.

As I moved through my teen years, my behavior with peers changed very little. Actively maintaining a narrow view of my world, as well as needing to control the environment so that I felt safe were both behavioral manifestations of Solar Plexus energy imbalances. While I acted out through my wardrobe and through my art, I was too afraid to do or say much more for many years. These repressed behaviors continued well into adulthood.

Although the energy of expression is Throat Chakrum territory, in active development later, it was being tapped into during my teens. At the time that my Solar Plexus was developing I needed expressive energy and so my Throat Chakrum engaged, contributed to, and was ultimately affected by the development of this lower Chakrum.

For me, this desire to look different grew from the sense that, deep down, there was something different about me. Actually, I used to say I thought something was "wrong" with me. To a certain degree I had decided to act and look different from others because I could not see the point of trying to fit into the popular, acceptable trends of that era. It was easy to dress like others but when I did, I often felt like a fraud.

Changes in my wardrobe temporarily eased my depression. Among family and friends, on the days when I felt too tired to try to change my mood, I would withdraw instead. Withdrawing made everything easier. When I was that depressed, it was easier to close in on myself and be quieter so that others would not notice me as much. By doing this I was also stifling my Solar Plexus energy, not allowing it to flow freely. All I knew was that I was hiding until I could breathe again. The mood I was in lifted and I could act like myself again.

While shutting down regularly meant that this energy was not allowed to fully develop, it also helped me avoid bringing attention to myself. In the context of my desire to act out through my wardrobe, rejecting invisibility, this is a contradiction. As a manifestation of an energy body imbalance, however, it is entirely consistent behavior.

If someone in my family interacted with me, which was nearly unavoidable, I had the tendency to sound and act cranky or moody. Acting fussy and being unable to tolerate interactions with others, even in the most pleasant circumstances, were regular manifestations of my Solar Plexus developing in an imbalanced way.

The truth was that the imbalances in my Root and Sacral Chakras were already siphoning energy away, and having to exert myself as my Solar Plexus was developing was exhausting me. Physiologically, the imbalances in my energy body were creating a sense of growing depression and, physically, this depression made me tired.

If withdrawing in order to rest and rebound from depression did not work and I had to interact with anyone, my tendency was to act as I felt. Somewhere deep down, I felt resentment because I had not been allowed to rest. If someone addressed me and I reacted with a bitter tone, I viewed it as their fault for interacting with me in the first place. They knew it would make me mad, so I allowed the anger to rise. The fact that I was often depressed meant that I was also often on the edge of anger. Hormonally, this is normal for any teenager. The thoughts that would pop into my head, when I was angry, however, were not normal.

When I felt anger, it frightened me. While I have many memories of times I was free to be creative, free to be myself and even times when I was depressed, I have few memories of being angry. That is not because it was rare. My memories from 5th to 12th grade may be much more intact than anything earlier, but something besides relief comes from realizing this. The more I attempt to recall certain relationships from that age, the more pockets of time I notice are lost. This, I believe, is because my negative emotions (anger, sadness, etc) were not being affirmed.

Any time that I disagreed with someone, stood up for myself, and realized they were still not listening or validating my point of view, the last thing I recall is feeling my anger bubbling up. Every time that happened, I felt invisible. Invisibility triggered my insecurity and fear. This pattern was created years earlier with each incident of abuse. As a teenager, then, my anger would regularly flip to something deeper and more frightening. My own anger often scared me to the degree that I could not remember back to what triggered me. The truth is as vivid as many of my memories are from those years of my life, I have little memory of people or situations I regularly felt anger toward.

There was a piece of me always ready to flip the switch from anger to rage. Feeling my anger rise, however, usually made me shut my mouth and try to stop the process. When I got angry, I reacted emotionally. With the addition of teenage hormones, controlling my behavior was no easy task. During these years, tears seemed to be on constant standby, ready to humiliate me in the presence of my siblings and friends. The moment I opened my mouth and expressed my emotional need, I was called "whiny" or "cranky". The accusations would fly between my siblings as a regular practice of taking sides. They would label it as 'joking around' and call me 'overdramatic' or 'oversensitive' when I shut down.

Had my Root and Sacral Chakras been allowed to develop into healthy energy centers, the development of personal power in my Solar Plexus would not have encountered so many roadblocks. The challenges presented by my siblings would not have affected me so deeply had my energetic and emotional foundation been strong before to heading into adolescence.

Well into adulthood, success and prosperity could not find a home in my energy body and therefore, my life. I doubted my own personal power, regardless of my extensive education and intense creativity, so all my Solar Plexus presented to the world was self-doubt as I took half-hearted shots at a better life.

An imbalanced Solar Plexus will affect all the other Chakras just as they affect the Solar Plexus in return. My self-doubt was supported by a clouded perception of reality. Perception is a function of Third Eye (6th) energy, a Chakrum that does not enter active development for decades. Though its energy was not developing at the same rate as my active Solar Plexus, it was directly affected by the regular shut down of this Chakrum. Because of this, my perception of my own personal power in the world remained imbalanced until I did work to heal it. If my energy body has an imbalance, then my perception of who I am, what I deserve, and what I am capable of, is also imbalanced.

One of the best things that happened while my Solar Plexus was actively developing was being invited to run on the cross-country team. From 7th to 12th grade, I was a long distance runner. Though I was the slowest runner on the team, it was a taste of freedom that no one could take away from me. The only person who could have tried was my coach and he remained supportive through every race, watching me finish last at nearly every event for those six years.

While I had a hard time breathing efficiently, I kept up my end of the bargain, training daily. Running long distance gave me the chance, regularly, to regain some of my personal power. The daily physical exertion became another outlet, joining with art making as a way to add balance to an era in my life that was otherwise remembered through a cloud of mild depression and bubbling anger.

Finding ways to strengthen this Chakrum helped me buy time until I was ready and able to start working on the cause of the imbalances. Deep down, I longed for enough time to find the answer. Once I found it, I thought, I would finally be able to be myself and live the life *I* wanted.

6

The 4th Chakrum: Heart

The Heart Chakrum, located in the center of the chest with its anatomical counterparts, the heart, lungs and thymus, is located under the sternum or breast bone. Of the seven Chakras, it is in the middle of the lineup. With three Chakras below it and three above, this one represents balance, equilibrium, and love.

The energy of the Heart Chakrum influences the diaphragm, and arms and hands, and lends energy to respiration, or breathing. Physiologically, imbalances take many forms. Asthma, high blood pressure, lung and heart disease, and issues related to compromised immune function (function of the thymus), are all possible manifestations of imbalances in Heart energy.

Behaviorally, this Chakrum drives growth, adaptability, caring and sharing in relationships with others, structure, routine and discipline, and personal growth. A strong Heart Chakrum makes it easy for you to find what you love to do and then pursue your personal dreams. This Chakrum enters active development in your 20's, a decade of great change. You are entering adulthood, seeking out jobs and partners and/or starting your own family.

Emotionally, when Heart energy is balanced you feel calm and clearheaded, patient and unthreatened by chaos in your world. You can act selflessly, empathize and have compassion without feeling restricted by your own unmet needs. You are able to set life goals and feel focused as you work toward fulfilling them. A strong Heart Chakrum enables you to live fully without feeling drained or threatened. When your Heart energy is balanced, you feel and act compassionately toward others without attachment. This means you are able to love yourself fully and then turn that love outward, able to embrace intimates, family, and the rest of the world without developing dependencies.

On the other hand, when your Heart energy is imbalanced, you may feel out of control or claustrophobic. You may feel trapped, isolated or otherwise oppressed. As a result, no matter what you try to do in the world, your life feels unfulfilled. Possessiveness and obsession grow out of this imbalance. The elements of balance and imbalance sound familiar, as previously developing Chakras involve similar relationships. In Heart energy, the need for balance becomes even more important because you are seeking the love you are designed to give and receive as part of the human experience.

Imbalances in the energy of the Heart are delicate, precarious, and energetically deep enough to cause great damage. Emotionally, the broken heart feels the most devastating. The energy of a broken heart is not relegated only to this Chakrum but affects all other Chakras, as well. As such, traumas that affect your Heart energy so deeply can cause a sort of energetic unraveling, sometimes resonating through your entire energy body. The pain felt in a broken Heart Chakrum, one that develops on top of an already imbalanced energy body, can affect you so deeply that it can feel like the Earth has momentarily stopped moving.

When it is imbalanced, Heart energy will seek relationships that provide constant reassurance to compensate for a lack of self-love and self-worth. Usually, this need surfaces because of unresolved issues in previous Chakrum and is being acted out in adulthood. This is a sign that there is room for healing.

You might reach out to another person for security as part of a relationship intended to be based in love and respect. Looking outside of yourself for emotional stability means you are depending on your partner to help you feel balanced. This type of energy exchange creates codependency. When codependent energy is present in a relationship, there is little opportunity for each personality to thrive and grow.

There is a difference between loving someone deeply and loving them dependently. Dependency, in Heart Chakrum terms, comes through as a loss of your identity in favor of catering to someone else's needs. This can happen in friendships and family relationships, as well as between intimate partners.

The more imbalances there are in the lower Chakras, the greater the chance your Heart Chakrum is also imbalanced. This may make you feel the need to find someone to be with so that you can feel better about yourself. Perhaps this person makes you feel more alive, joyful, confident or attractive. Seeking companionship in this manner probably means you are seeking another energy body to supplement your own. Many of us do this because we have a difficult time feeling alive, joyful, confident or attractive by ourselves. Many of us do this because we do not enjoy being alone.

What secrets were being kept by my Heart Chakrum?

When it began active development, my Heart energy had unstable ground to stand on. In my 20s, my primary purpose for living became finding companionship. Though I wished I could find higher paying jobs, the need to find someone to make my life better eclipsed my desire to find a fulfilling career. I thought if I could find someone to love me despite how I felt about myself then I would feel protected, accepted, and supported. For me that meant I could then stop worrying about my debt and would be free to focus on turning my life around. Truth be told, I wanted someone to take over because deep down I had essentially given up faith in my own ability to turn my life around. I wanted someone to save me.

Energetically, though my Heart energy had not begun full development until after my teen years had passed, it had energy flowing through it. This meant that, like all other parts of my energy body, my Heart Chakrum had sustained wounds from the sexual abuse that happened while my Root and Sacral Chakras were developing.

At the end of college, having not met anyone yet, I looked back on my life and realized I had never really been asked out on a date. During high school I was invited to a Homecoming or Prom by someone whose friends were going. Occasionally, a romantic attachment would begin to develop but my own painful shyness would soon contribute to its demise. So much of my energy had been focused on 'future-tripping' about the unpredictability of such relationships that adolescence, and then college, had passed by with no companionship to show for it.

In college I gave myself few opportunities because I feared socializing off campus. Most people I knew had gotten fake ids in the first week and spent every subsequent weekend at a local bar. Some of them got to know each other really, really fast. Having stayed back at the dorm, I would later hear the stories of their near misses, heartbreaks and, sometimes, victimization.

All of those adventures were the result of college co-eds seeking companionship. Some hoped for temporary hookups, others had their hopes set on finding love. I avoided all of that. Suddenly, I found myself comforted by the fact that my irrational fears and need for control of my surroundings had steered me clear of the dangers into which others fell.

In my 20s, personal ads were not yet considered trendy, but I saw them as my only option. I was free to create my own image and safely bring attention to myself, controlling the environment each step of the way. I placed my own and, sometimes, answered others. Looking back over that decade, I had short-lived relationships with a handful of men, one at a time. None of them could survive the emotional instability inherent in the pairing. It was no consolation to see their need for companionship was coming from a similar source. There were other, equally short connections with women along the way, none of which succeeded because they also had their own emotional imbalances.

From a decade of searching, the one that had the greatest impact on me was also one of the shortest. A man I dated for two months introduced me to codependency. The first month was blissful, filled with lingering conversations and lengthy emails. From the beginning, not a day passed without extensive contact.

My energy body was walking wounded. His energy body was wounded, as well. When I met him, my Heart energy was in full swing, though imbalanced. My energy body was reaching out, open and vulnerable, and his was reaching out to me.

During that first month of loving emails and conversations, we had reassured each other of how wonderful, beautiful, talented, creative, and amazing the other was. It was the perfect match of codependent energies, two broken souls finding their mate. When I accepted his energy, offered in the form of such reassurance, it gave my Heart Chakrum more energy. I was not aware of how wounded I was. When he accepted my energy it was equally reassuring to him. Together, we functioned very well.

Unbeknownst to me, I was learning how it felt to give my energy away. My perception, however, was that I was falling in love because it felt like nothing I had ever experienced. Being with him made me happier than I had ever been. I had glimpses of such joy before but they were fleeting. A month full of drama, passion, and a sense of constantly needing him and being needed by him had clouded my judgment. When I was in the middle of it, I thought it would last forever. In hindsight, however, the bubble bursting seemed inevitable.

As we entered the second month, I started to feel a bit smothered. We went out to dinner and I mustered up the courage to tell him that I was trying to make a decision about my future, my career, and needed more time for myself. It had taken me nearly a week to summon the courage to tell him because I had been so afraid that he would break up with me for putting my needs first. His normally gentle, loving countenance suddenly shifted, though he did not get angry. While I was unaware of the energy body at the time, I remember feeling the air shift somehow. He had yet to say a word but I already had the feeling something was coming.

That was when he informed me that, actually, he had recently gone out with his ex-girlfriend and had been battling the feeling, ever since, that he was still in love with her. My energy body was so imbalanced that this news felt like a sucker punch.

Moments like this are dramatic enough without the additional burden of an imbalanced energy body. When emotions exist in such an environment events can feel much more dramatic than they might actually be. My perception was skewed by an energy imbalance and created a new emotional vocabulary for me. Instead of feeling disappointed if I was passed over for a job, I felt judged and then devastated. Instead of feeling deep sadness from a breakup, I felt worthless, like it was the end of the world.

Sitting across from him, everything immediately changed. Within seconds, I felt a sharp pain in my chest that felt like I had been stabbed. Physiologically, my skin felt like it was on fire. Years later I was told the sharp pain may have been the beginning of a panic attack. Because my Heart Chakrum was so weak, I did not experience a full attack. Instead, I went numb. The sharp pain was the last physical sensation I had for many weeks. The message I came away with was a very old one. Standing up for me meant I would get hurt. This time, my heart was broken. Though it was a brief, two-month relationship, it took me two years to feel ready to try again.

As I entered my early 30s, I learned that I could not physically feel true love, compassion or empathy for another person until I directed it toward myself. At the time that first memory surfaced, I did not feel the need to immediately know the details of what had happened in order to realize that I deserved much more out of life than I had settled for. Once I started studying my life and journaling my way through the related emotions, I started feeling something new - love for myself. Slowly, consistently, I started living life differently.

At first, healing seemed to cause loneliness. As I kept focusing, however, I was able to recognize loneliness as an emotional manifestation of energy that was ready to be let go. When I extended my Heart energy to myself, first, I broke an old pattern.

Putting my needs first caused a shift in my energy body. I was feeding my own Heart Chakrum and, as a result, I noticed that I cared less and less about finding companionship and intimacy. Though part of my energy body was still yearning for someone to distract me, every day I re-dedicated myself to studying my abusive past and changing my existing behaviors. As time passed, the most delightful thing started happening.

By focusing on myself, I turned all my energy inward. This meant I was no longer straining myself by overextending my energy to others. This reversal in direction allowed others to find and approach me, instead. New partnerships entered my life. Having decided that my healing was more important than having intimacy, I found myself making new friends. These friends were healers, themselves, and were in various states of intentionally changing their own lives. I traded work with them, simultaneously teaching and learning new techniques. From these trades, my professional confidence blossomed. That was surprising to me because I already had a sense of pride in my work.

Those healing trades taught me something extraordinary. The energy body I was born with was never destroyed by the abuse I sustained. Sometimes my energy body recoiled for protection, other times it was piled upon and shoved aside to make room for energy of the people who victimized me. As I released the energy of heart break, victimization and trauma, my own energy body was able to rise from its shrunken, crouched position and begin to stretch out.

I no longer needed someone to come in and coax me out of my darkness. Support from friends, old and new, helped me as I renewed my sense of self-love and self-respect. I felt strengthened by them as I found my own way, without dependency. I did not feel loneliness. Relieved, I took a deep breath and noticed that something felt different.

Physiologically, my Heart energy had strengthened enough that I was able to breathe into my belly, exercising my diaphragm for the first time in years. The diaphragm, affected by Heart energy, pulls the lower lungs down, expanding the amount of space available for oxygen to enter the body. In childhood, fear and anxiety closed down my Heart Chakrum almost completely and kept it closed for years. This had a direct impact on my breathing.

I had been a shallow breather, inhaling only into my upper chest. At some point in my past, I had learned that breathing with my diaphragm would initiate or intensify feelings of anxiety. This was something I regularly avoided because it made me feel out of control.

This time, when I started using my diaphragm to breathe, I felt soreness in my lungs. They were receiving oxygen in corners and crevices that had not been accessed in a long time. I also felt odd, mild sensations in my chest. My heart muscle and lung tissue felt very weak. I had to work hard to concentrate on this new way of breathing. Physically, the soreness felt like it was coming from parts of my heart and lungs that had never been used before. My energy body had been protecting those parts for a long time. My other Chakras were on the mend which allowed my Heart energy to expand and stretch. I could finally…breathe.

7

The 5th Chakrum: Throat

The energy of the Throat Chakrum is designed for expression: for speaking up, having your voice heard, making an impact in the world. In Western culture, we stifle a great deal of energy in our Throat Chakras. Perhaps this is because, socially, we place a tremendous amount of importance on being accepted by others. Many of us choose to keep quiet and allow others to speak, even when they are not fully representing our own wishes. By our silence, however, we are stifling our own energy flow.

This does not mean we have to speak up all the time. It does mean, however, that we ought to be giving ourselves a daily outlet for our voices and experiences. This can be done through journaling/keeping a diary, spending time talking with friends, art making, therapy sessions, or other activities where we are honestly expressing ourselves in a comfortable, non-judgmental environment.

91

Energy in the Throat Chakrum affects the function of everything from the ears to the upper chest, the thyroid and parathyroid glands, the trachea and cervical (neck) vertebrae, temporomandibular joint (TMJ), nose and ears, and mouth (including lips, teeth, and gums). In human development this part of your energy body is actively developing in your 30s.

Throat Chakrum energy flows through all forms of expression. Physiologically, mechanisms that are affected by the Throat Chakrum include everything you use to communicate. By 'communicate', I am including body language. The human body is meant to move in space. You may know people who 'talk with their hands' and there are many cultures in which body language is the primary form of communication. Using your body to accentuate your words is often a way to be more persuasive. When you tell someone how you feel, they do not need to respond verbally for you to know their reaction. A tilt of the head, stiffening of the shoulders, or a smile, is all you need.

Body language is not restricted to the visual plane. Those who are visually impaired or blind may be able to feel a shift in energy despite the fact that they cannot see the body stiffen or see the nuances in a facial expression.

One detail that makes one person completely different from the next is their voice. Each human voice is like a fingerprint. We are meant to speak up, to make our voices heard. How many of us actually do this? Socially, it is often considered a risk to speak up in a crowd. If you do speak your mind, you are inviting response and reaction from your audience.

When your audience does respond, it will stimulate your energy body. What if someone disagrees with what you have said and speaks up, challenging you? Perhaps you respond calmly and find yourself engaged in healthy debate (balanced Throat energy). Maybe you have to elaborate, speaking more vigorously because they were not listening to what you said and are actually just being argumentative (again, balanced). Perhaps, though, you feel attacked by their response and you panic, wanting to disengage from the exchange, regretting that you spoke up in the first place (imbalanced Throat energy).

You may know someone (or be someone) who has no hesitation about speaking up. If your communication style is calm and you invite response and discussion, healthy energy is flowing through your Throat Chakrum. If, however, you find that you often feel argumentative, accusatory, or regularly raise your voice, then your Throat energy is probably imbalanced.

If emotions and behaviors related to this Chakrum have gone unaddressed and unresolved, your energy body is going to manifest the imbalance physically. Most often when pain or stiffness is felt in the neck area, something is being stifled. Either you are not allowed to speak up or you are holding yourself back. Energy is stopped up in your neck. Anything that causes physical pain or illness in this region of the body is directly related to expression and having your voice heard.

Throat Chakrum imbalances take many forms. As for the dysfunctions that manifest physically, when this Chakrum is imbalanced, a myriad of issues can develop. Problems with the throat and neck include soreness, scratchiness, or stiff neck muscles you dismiss as 'sleeping on it wrong'. Other physiological issues can include under- or over-active thyroid, ear problems, laryngitis or tonsillitis. In the extreme, Throat energy imbalances may contribute to thyroid carcinomas. The thyroid gland produces hormones that regulate general metabolism as well as specific calcium metabolism in bone cells. This means it has a direct relationship with the activity of the skeletal system.

The respiratory system is also affected by imbalance in the Throat Chakrum. This often manifests as shallow, uneven breathing which can lead to tightness and soreness in the muscles of the neck and upper chest. These muscles are responsible for lifting the rib cage so the upper lungs can fill with oxygen.

In the energy body, individual Chakras often partner with others. Sometimes, the partnerships are fruitful. The Throat Chakrum, for instance, often works with the Sacral to boost create output and expression. Other Chakrum partnerships serve an entirely different purpose. When considering imbalances in the Throat Chakrum, it is important to account for its relationship with each of the lower Chakras. There might be an imbalance in the lower Chakras that the Throat is trying very hard to express, though it has its own limited energy flow.

Sometimes one Chakrum must feed off of another to compensate for specific weaknesses. In my experience, it is common for individuals with stifled Throat energy to also have imbalances in their Root and/or Sacral Chakras. This partnership manifests through emotions and behaviors. An example is feeling insecure (Root imbalance) to the degree that you are too afraid to express yourself. Future-tripping about others' response and possible negative judgments (Sacral imbalance) might also dampen your desire to speak your mind.

When the Throat and other Chakras are in this type of compensating partnership, it is often the result of energy in the Throat Chakrum being traumatized at the time the lower Chakras (Root or Sacral) were actively developing. Fear of being judged, feelings of inadequacy (Sacral), feeling unsafe or insecure (Root), are all reasons why some people do not speak up or stand up for themselves. In this book, I am not taking into account social structures, in many parts of the world, where individuals who speak out are literally risking their lives.

Behaviorally, a healthy Throat Chakrum contributes to a strong voice, confidence in what you have said after you have said it, and a willingness to continue expressing yourself. Inherent in that willingness is taking responsibility for everything you say and do. When you express yourself, you are taking a great risk. The risk is that you will be judged for what you have said or done. You may not feel that doing those things are risks at all. If so, your Throat Chakrum is probably quite healthy.

However, if you do feel that expressing yourself is risky and each time you do it you have to gather the willpower, your Throat energy may be imbalanced. You may be afraid or unsure of the consequences of speaking up and telling your truth.

While the Throat is only one of seven described in this book, in my experience it is one of two (the other is the Third Eye) that will provide the answers you need when you are healing your energy body. The Throat Chakrum is a powerful energy center because it gives a voice to all the other Chakras.

Personally, I find the most powerful way to keep my Throat Chakrum energy healthy is by journaling. Initially, self-examination through journaling taught me that I was the only one who could do this healing work, make these changes in my life. When I was ready, I began journaling so that I could release all the things that were weighing me down. I could not have predicted how quickly my life would begin to change, or how dramatic those changes would be.

What secrets were held in my Throat Chakrum?

When I was two years old, there was energy flowing in my Throat Chakrum. Though it would not enter active development until my 30s, it was still susceptible to trauma and injury. At the time, I was physically abused because I was ill and crying. The physical abuse made me stop crying. That incident taught me that expressing me was bad. My Throat Chakrum was temporarily shut down.

When I was three, my life was threatened as a way to keep me quiet. My energy body translated that as a reminder to keep my Throat Chakrum shut off. Many additional incidents over the next few years incorporated threats and sexual abuse to maintain my silence. Once I learned the lesson enough times, I began stifling myself. While my abusers originally forced my Throat energy to shut down, soon I took over and kept myself quiet, insuring my own safety.

When I was three, the specific abuse I sustained was oral molestation. For adult survivors of sexual abuse, this often manifests years in later years as oral fixation. Emotional instability triggers comforting hand-to-mouth behavior. Such behavior can include eating, smoking, drinking, chewing (fingernails, gum, pens, etc), sucking (straws, lollipops), biting (children act this out more commonly than adults), or any number of other activities.

I had already learned to use food as a tool for comfort, and had picked up nail biting along the way to supplement when food was unavailable. My eating and nail biting devolved into regular vices for use whenever I was feeling anxious or depressed. These were sensations I had when I felt neglected or invisible, or, conversely, exposed and vulnerable.

I reached for food or bit my nails for comfort and distraction. Sometimes I did these things just to stuff something into my mouth, literally silencing myself. There were a string of such incidents, all of which ultimately led to significant weight gain. These behaviors prove that early childhood trauma affected my energy body. While this Chakrum would not begin active development for almost 30 years, most of those years in the meantime were spent meeting the needs of my severely traumatized Throat energy.

While I had little or no energy flowing in my Throat Chakrum during my teen years, my other Chakras had enough juice in them to help me pursue a love of art making. As a teenager, I produced my first large scale painting during a summer program. It was a full body, nearly life-size, self-portrait from behind. I painted it in triptych format – one image painted across three separate panels of plywood. I hung them horizontally, one above another, and separated each panel from the next by one inch. I was, literally, painting myself in pieces.

I was afraid to try painting realistically, which would have required intricate details and textures. I painted my long brown hair and clothing with little detail. A variety of materials were used to fill the space surrounding my body including twigs, pieces of broken mirror, and old candles I used to melt wax onto the surface.

The twigs, melted wax, and mirror fragments were all affixed in various places in the space around my hair and dress. I had glued at least one piece of mirror directly on my torso. At the time I made this painting, I had no memory of surviving abuse.

Though imbalanced, my Solar Plexus (personal power) and Sacral (creativity) Chakras had enough combined energy to motivate me to paint this piece. The day I brought this triptych painting home from that workshop was the day it went into storage in the basement, one panel stacked in front of the next, against the wall.

Recently, I visited my mother's basement, where this painting is stored. I was surprised to see that, in the center of my back, I had affixed a large chunk of broken mirror in the exact location of the Solar Plexus Chakrum. I had remembered intending to hang the painting on the wall so that the mirror would be at the viewer's eye level. I was inviting everyone who looked at my painting to see themselves as my power source. I was powerless without them. My Solar Plexus and Sacral Chakras had pooled resources so that I could express what was really going on in my energy body.

Though my Throat Chakrum had little or no energy flowing through it at the time, my actively developing Solar Plexus had enough energy to power my art creation. Art was safe because I could express myself and temporarily relieve some of my depression. At the same time, I could avoid telling anyone how I really felt or what my art actually meant.

While my energy body was trying to keep the trauma suppressed by bingeing, nail biting, and art making, these behaviors could not maintain balance long-term. This meant that my energy was overloaded and my body had no choice but to manifest some stress physically. First, a thyroid problem was diagnosed and, a few years later, a cyst developed on the back of my neck. I had to overcome my shame and embarrassment (Sacral imbalance) and ask for help (Throat) from doctors to get these issues resolved.

Even in adulthood, well into my 20s, I had a difficult time expressing myself and my needs. Most of the time I waited until someone else said what I wanted to say, and then I would agree with them. It felt safest to speak up that way. When I did choose to speak up first, I would be so nervous that I could not breathe easily for a long time afterward.

Eventually, the anxiety I felt about using my voice compounded what my body was already repressing, causing additional physical problems. In my mid-twenties I had cysts removed near and on my tailbone. This is Root Chakrum territory. The energy in my Root had been blocked for twenty years. I could not use my voice to release the energy and ultimately required outpatient surgery to fix what had manifested physically.

A few years after all the cysts were removed, I found myself in Reiki training, learning the energy-based reasons why those cysts developed in the first place. I was in training just as my Throat Chakrum was beginning active development. My teachers had discovered that, along with all the other imbalances in my energy body, my Throat Chakrum was energetically 'dead'. This meant that there was no energy flowing through it.

When I began training in Reiki, memories of abuse had not yet surfaced, so there was nothing to actively stifle. Once my teachers sensed a lack of energy in my Throat Chakrum, they focused on balancing my energy body. Soon after, energy began flowing into and through my Throat. Behaviorally, as energy flowing through my body evened out, I felt the urge to journal. Also, though I had not painted in many years, I felt compelled to return to art making.

Journaling and painting were safe forms of expression because they were private activities. Privacy insured that I would be able to express myself but remain in hiding, still fearful of bringing attention to myself. Embarrassment, inadequacy, fear of judgment, and avoidance of intimate relationships guaranteed continued security as I started living with a newly balanced Chakra System. Changes in energy are often soft, subtle. Though my energy body was suddenly balanced and, for the moment, fully functional, it did not mean I was immediately able to change everything and live a new life.

Changes in behavior were not so sudden that they were jarring. It felt more like I had new ideas more often than I was used to, and that I had been injected with a bit of energy to try them out. When I began journaling, I was suddenly noticing so much about myself and the world that it felt like there was never enough time to write it all down. Feeling motivated was refreshing and exhausting at the same time. I did not immediately notice that my depression had lifted because I was still physically tired.

Before my energy was balanced, the lack of flow in my Throat had stifled activity in my Third Eye and Crown, as well. My Throat Chakrum was reopened just as it was entering active development. Simultaneously, things started "occurring to me" on a regular basis. By opening my Throat Chakrum, the next Chakrum to develop had also been stimulated. In those moments, I was connected to my gut instinct, energy of the Third Eye.

Soon after I began journaling, I found I was writing at length about patterns I noticed in my emotions and behaviors. I noticed those same behaviors reflected back to me in my relationships. As soon as I saw the patterns, I realized I had a choice and could make changes if I really wanted to. It did not take much to convince me.

This run of thoughts and inspiration was a combination of Third Eye (instinct) and Crown energy (Divine inspiration). The first thing that crossed my mind was that it would be a great time to start documenting my life. Until that moment, I had been convinced that my life was not important enough to bear witness to. The next thing that occurred to me was that I should write a book about my experience.

These days, some of my most empowering moments are the result of journaling. I am grateful for having rediscovered my voice. Inspiration to write and paint now comes easily. Opening my Throat Chakrum enabled my Heart, Solar Plexus, Sacral and Root Chakras to return to their own spaces. Those energy shifts, in turn, brought up more bits of memory and chances to heal.

This was the most difficult chapter to write. Finishing this chapter meant that I successfully stood up to the threats on my life and the physical and sexual abuse. Using my strong, balanced Throat Chakrum energy means that I can now tell my story. The consequences of telling the truth are heady, difficult, and necessary.

Writing this book was the first literary project to come out of my healing Throat Chakrum. My intention was to write about my experience and explain how healing is possible no matter what hand life has dealt you, and regardless of the choices you made because of that hand. Healing and change start the moment you decide it is time.

The Throat Chakrum is the center of energy fueling your vocal and expressive fingerprints. Behaviorally, having it stifled or silenced is equivalent to having the meaning knocked out of your life. As humans, we have a voice not only for interpersonal communication, but also so that we can share our unique experiences with the world. It is an important mechanism in our evolution.

You may have lost track of your voice, whether it was silenced by others or by yourself. When the time comes to tell your story, your Throat Chakrum will be ready. What will it take for you to break your silence?

8

The 6th Chakrum: Third Eye

The sixth Chakrum, also known as the Third Eye, does not begin active development until mid-life. This Chakrum is located on the forehead, between the eyebrows, and has also been called the Brow Chakrum. It is responsible for energy related to intuition, perception, sensing and knowing. In contrast to the outward expression of the Throat Chakrum, this Chakrum actively looks inward.

The energy flowing through the Third Eye supports intellectual activity including the ability to analyze and draw conclusions. It also supports the shift from intellectual activity to intuitive awareness – having a gut feeling, trusting and following it without analysis or intellectual processing. Activities fueled by Third Eye energy include a belief in the intangible, such as faith in a higher power; the ability to sense other dimensions beyond our known reality; and the ability to detach from space and time. This detachment allows us to connect more deeply with our own insight and intuition.

When the energy body is healthy, the lower Chakras - Root, Sacral, and Solar Plexus - contribute to the physical health of the human body and are strongly affected by our human experiences. The middle Chakras - Heart and Throat – while still connected to the physical health of the human body, are also somewhat connected to the spiritual health of the human *being*. The upper Chakras - Third Eye and Crown – while connected to the human body are also strongly connected to the energies outside our physical selves: the intangible, the spiritual.

There is no way to have a healthy Third Eye Chakrum if there are dysfunctions and imbalances in the Chakras below. As more balance is restored in the lower Chakras, more clarity can be restored in this Chakrum. The Third eye enables us to *see* clearly. By *see*, I mean *intuit*.

Your intuition is as unique to you as your human experience. While similar ideas may occur to you as occur to others in touch with their intuition, the messages you receive are ultimately as unique as your voice and your fingerprint. It is not dictated by your behaviors, nor is it influenced by how you have lived your life in the past. Heeding your intuition will only steer you in the direction of your highest purpose, your highest good.

When imbalances exist in those lower Chakras, the energy in the Third Eye may be strained. A common behavioral manifestation of Third Eye imbalance is regularly second guessing your instincts. When this Chakrum is imbalanced, it can also be difficult to have a linear thought process, making it almost impossible to think straight. You may feel like you are caught running in mental circles; you may find it difficult to stop analyzing situations because you are anxious or worried about the outcome. It may be hard to make decisions about practical or mundane things because you feel distracted or flighty. Quieting your mind enough to allow for intuition, insight, and sensitivity is nearly impossible when Third Eye energy is blocked or imbalanced.

If you have an imbalance in your Third Eye Chakrum, your self-perception may be skewed. This can manifest in the notion that no matter what, you must always do things perfectly. Such standards are almost impossible to meet, causing you to feel disappointed in yourself regularly. Over time, if unresolved, this may extend to your relationships.　You may silently project too high a level of expectations on those closest to you, again causing disappointment when such standards are not met.

Physiologically, the energy of the Third Eye influences the eyes, ears, nose, sinuses, lower brain, and the endocrine and nervous systems.　Energy flow through the Third Eye also influences the pituitary gland.　This gland is directly related to Thyroid function which means it is also influenced, albeit indirectly, by Throat Chakrum energy.　Energy imbalances can cause visual disturbances, headaches, and nightmares.　Often, imbalances elsewhere in the energy body can result in a gut feeling that something is off, though you cannot put your finger on exactly what it is.　When this happens, it is possible that there is an imbalance in your body, energetically or physically, and your Third Eye is the messenger.

What secrets did my Third Eye hold?

I spent most of my life dismissing my intuition.　Though I learned how to listen to my gut in massage school and, later, in Reiki training, it has taken many years of practice to truly follow my instincts.　As an adult, specifically during my 20's, this meant that I regularly regretted decisions I made and had to accept the consequences. Consequences came regularly. I spent money I did not have which increased my debt load. I engaged in emotionally harmful or neglectful relationships, each of which led to codependency and loneliness. Rather than go with my gut and make life-changing decisions, I consistently second-guessed myself and made decisions that did not serve my highest good...or any good at all.

By regularly ignoring my intuition, I had been maintaining behaviors that did not allow for spiritual or emotional growth. It was comforting to me to maintain this stagnation because it kept life predictable. Pre-existing imbalances in my lower Chakras supported my need to control my surroundings, to maintain such predictability in my daily life.

Using intuition as a guide, on the other hand, led me to new experiences, more happiness and growth. This resulted in permanent life change. When I remembered the first abuse incident and memories that were once repressed began trickling in, my gut feeling was that I better write it all down. My instinct compelled me to journal regularly. Soon, it became obvious that writing was going to meet two needs I did not realize I had. The first was that I needed a place to document all the pieces of memory that were surfacing so I would not have to try to remember every detail later on. The second was to have a place to unload all the emotions that were stirred up along with the memories.

Journal after journal filled up in a way I had not expected. While I had started writing because I thought all of my lost memories might surface all at once, the time between one bit of memory surfacing and the next would sometimes stretch over weeks or months. My energy body was allowing memory to surface that slowly because it was all I could mentally and emotionally handle.

Each time I wrote down what was weighing on me, the clearer my Third Eye became. Insights as a result of journaling helped me to see the possibility of change in my life. Childhood abuse had planted strong seeds, practically guaranteeing that my behavior, as an adult, would be dysfunctional. Once energy was flowing regularly through this Chakrum, however, I was able to understand that my emotions and behaviors were symptoms and not the source of dysfunction, themselves. Instinct told me that in order to make change and begin healing, I would first have to feel the reality of my circumstances in my Heart Chakrum. This was a painful, necessary exercise that brought relief soon afterward. My Heart energy had to release its dependence on these unhealthy behaviors. The next project was to understand that I was worthy of much more in all areas of my life, and to practice feeling that in my Heart Chakrum, as well. Through all of this, my Third Eye showed me that I was ready to learn self-love.

Once I faced imbalances in my professional and personal life, my gut delivered an even more intimate lesson. Months had passed and I found myself journaling about food. A lifelong behavioral issue, I finally admitted that I was avoiding difficult emotions by eating. Food was my only guaranteed source of love and comfort, so admitting this even in a journal was a sign that change was on the way.

One of the ways I recognize intuition is when something *occurs to me* or *crosses my mind*. At the moment I accepted my avoidance behavior, it crossed my mind that my abuse history was at the root of my struggle with obesity. That was an epiphany. The idea came through so clearly that it was easy to accept. It was the answer I needed in order to start seriously losing weight.

Permanent progress toward a healthier, lighter physical body started that day. Balanced, healthy Third Eye energy flow had opened communication between my physical body, its related Chakras, and my gut sensitivity. By listening to my intuition I was learning how to heal a part of my physical health that, historically, made me feel most out of control.

The more I wrote down, the clearer my Third Eye became. New ideas and inspiration came occurred to me regularly. With this inspiration came energy and motivation like I had never felt before. One day it occurred to me that I could not remember the last time I felt depressed.

It turned out that as long as I was writing down what was weighing on my mind and heart, my energy body was no longer holding onto any of it. That meant room was available for much needed relief. This made space for more joy and happiness, inspiration and opportunity.

I have found that the key to working with the energy of my Third Eye Chakrum is to be patient with myself and to understand that my gut, my instinct, will never steer me wrong. *The key is to trust myself.*

What would clarity in your Third Eye enable *you* to see?

9

The 7th Chakrum: Crown

The Crown is the 7th major Chakrum in the energy body and is the one that connects us to all of creation, including the energy of the Divine. This Chakrum is the conduit that allows energy from the greater Universe to flow through us.

The Crown is located at the center of the top of your head, extending upward from your physical body into the energy field of the outside world. Physiologically, Crown Chakrum energy affects the eyes, the function of the Pineal gland and is associated with higher brain functions. When this Chakrum is balanced, it allows us to understand and become more intuitive to the pulse of the world around us.

The intuitive sense from the Crown Chakrum is similar in feeling to that of the Third Eye. The Third Eye helps us heal ourselves as it guides us into our higher purpose as individuals. The purpose of the Crown, then, is to guide us toward understanding and connecting with Spirit, the Divine within. This connection enables us to feel empathy and understanding of others and the world. Such a profound spiritual understanding can feel like it has been disconnected when there is an imbalance in the Crown Chakrum.

Once self-healing is in process, however, the Third Eye can boost the ability of the Crown to sense what is really motivating those around us. The energy of the Crown Chakrum enables a deeper understanding of the world we live in, simultaneously hinting at the ever elusive meaning of life.

The energy of the Crown Chakrum begins flowing, along with the rest of the energy body, when the Root begins active development, in utero. Your Crown Chakrum enters its own active development when you enter mid-life. In Western culture, this is the age of what is commonly known as the mid-life crisis. You may feel lost spiritually, are beginning to sense your own mortality, and/or you are realizing that you have lived your entire adult life in the service of others at the expense of your own needs, desires, and, perhaps, your own spirit.

As the Crown enters active development, it is possible that your behavior will change in a noticeable way. Often, this is noticeable because it directly affects those around you. If you were accustomed to putting the needs of others, whether partner and children, elders, or other relationships, before your own, you may suddenly feel compelled to reverse your priorities. You may feel an internal pull, an itch to meet your own needs first. This pull may be impossible to dismiss or ignore. This change in behavior can be shocking. You may not know where the urge came from, only that you feel unable to ignore it. Being unable to explain your motivation can cause breakdowns in communication with loved ones.

Crown Chakrum energy imbalances can manifest in a number of other ways, as well. Imbalances in this Chakrum manifest, physiologically, as higher brain malfunctions from migraines to problems with physical coordination. Imbalances can also manifest as feelings of lethargy, depression, and an inability to focus or concentrate when trying to learn something new.

Just as lower Chakrum imbalances affect higher Chakras, when higher Chakras begin active development they will affect the balance of lower Chakras. As the Crown Chakrum is entering development, imbalances in the lower Chakras will be shaken up. Spiritual connection, whether internally, with others, or with the Divine, is the result of a powerful energy shift. These connections will not be strong unless your energy body is balanced. As with every part of the energy body, healing and restoring balance is possible anytime in human development.

What secrets did my Crown Chakrum hold for me?

As I lived with mild depression, one thing was underneath it all. I felt abandoned by God. The God I learned about in Catholic schools was supposed to bless the suffering and the meek. I was suffering and felt meek most of the time but did not feel blessed at all. The depression and the specific sense of spiritual abandonment were both caused, in part, by an imbalance in my Crown Chakrum.

I was raised in an upper middle class household, so I was a child of privilege, but that lifestyle did not make me feel blessed. Despite living in a comfortable home, having food on the table, and all the resources I needed, I did not feel blessed in the way I thought God would provide – feeling happy, joyful, loving, and inspired. I rarely felt a connection to God, except during the holidays. That time of year renewed my hope that something could change. Overall, however, it was a time of year that I could revel in distractions, forgetting my depression for awhile. Lower Chakrum imbalances were tugging at the energy in my Crown, so there was no room for healthy energy flow. At the time, I did not have any idea how much healing I needed to do.

I was raised Catholic, attended Catholic schools and even graduated from a Jesuit university. During college, I experienced the first of two educational crises. I was studying the only thing I was passionate about, fine arts, but could already sense that it would not lead me to the financially successful future I thought would make life easier. In the past, I used church as a refuge, a place to rest and hide from stress and depression. During college, however, the church I attended was on campus so there was no true respite from my worries. Already feeling so lost, I translated this lack of refuge as "God" no longer caring about me. I decided that since I was apparently not worth "His" time, "He" was no longer worth mine. I became officially disillusioned with the Catholic Church, stopped attending services, and stopped praying.

Somewhere deep inside I still desired a spiritual connection, but I rejected the idea of the Catholic God on such a deep level that I thought my only option was to cut the cord and start fresh.

Calling a higher power "God" was, in my mind, a Catholic label. I decided this "God" was one tier below the Absolute, so walking away from "God" did not mean I was giving up. It enabled me to cut "God" out and make room for another connection to take "His" place. I either needed to find a different symbolic spiritual entity or I needed to figure out how to make a direct connection with the Absolute. Since I felt abandoned by "Him", I thought it would be really easy to sever the ties and start fresh.

I was seeking God on a cognitive level so that I would not have to feel the heavy sensation that had been growing in my heart. If there really was no higher power loving me and protecting me, I honestly thought there was no point to living. Though I was not emotionally strong enough to handle the fact that there might be no "God", intellectually, I felt compelled...desperate to find one. Though my Crown Chakrum was imbalanced, there was enough energy to support this journey because it was so limited in scope – driven only by mental activity.

My plan for finding a connection with a different higher power was not as limited as my ability to deal with the information I was going to be exposed to. This restriction was partially because of my existing need to have the God from my childhood SEE me and finally SAVE me. With that energy leading the way, it was unlikely that I would find anything that would satisfy me. Still, I intended to try very hard.

I had been taught that Catholicism was exclusive and Protestant religions were somehow more diluted in their practices. Given this prejudice, my first stop was going to be Protestant-land. I attended a Lutheran service, and then one at a Presbyterian church. They still called their higher power "God" but they weren't Catholic, so I had hope.

The buildings that housed the services, however, lacked artistic and architectural significance for me. There were no statues or other visual distractions, which I had been taught was somewhat the point of Protestantism. I was immediately bored. I was still too close to the "God" I grew up with. There was simply less of "Him" represented on the walls and around the altars in those churches. I decided to leave Christianity behind and found myself at a Buddhist temple.

The interior was full of sculpture, dripping in rich reds and golds, and the floor was covered in beautiful cushions to sit on. There was a discussion at the end of the meditation service so that attendees could ask questions. One individual asked if it is possible to believe in God and be Buddhist. She was told a flat, but gentle, *no*. The sense of exclusion was familiar. It was too similar to my Catholic past and I had to say goodbye to them, as well. I had gone to these places with the hope that one would instantly gratify me. None of them did during my first visit so I did not return. By acting out of emotional necessity rather than spiritual desire I was not giving them a chance.

I had gone to the Lutheran, Presbyterian and Buddhist services to find communities that would inspire me the way the stained glass windows, paintings and sculptures of the Catholic Church once did. I found none of that. I still heard group chanting, singing and saw interactions between people who might then ignore each other outside of the service until the next week. Nothing was different except the visual stimulation.

I even tried a new Catholic Church. They did not kneel as often as I remembered, but everything else was the same. Men played the lead roles. The art around the interior of the church was the same. The things they were chanting were so familiar that, before I knew what was happening, my own voice joined the others. It was like riding a bicycle, which would have been comforting had I not noticed I had a strange sensation building in me. I realized that I felt like a stranger in an environment that I used to feel at home in. Even the art couldn't hold my attention. I felt terrible. This particular church proved to me that I could not go back where I came from. It was a very lonely feeling.

At the same time that I was actively seeking a spiritual safe haven, I continued to struggle financially and had an excess of emotional needs. I was getting very tired of it all, so I took a break and hoped that something would change without me trying to change it.

Most of this spiritual journey happened when I was in graduate school. At the time, I was experiencing another educational crisis. Having a Fine Arts degree and no self-confidence in my own creativity meant I made no attempts to make a living from my own work. As a result, I held down low paying jobs while I tried to figure out what my next move should be.

I had enrolled in classes, occasionally, trying to decide whether to pursue graduate school. Having little confidence in my own ability to turn passion into a career, I chose instead to follow the lead of family and friends. I enrolled in graduate school to become a teacher because that career brought stability to the lives of nearly everyone I knew. A couple of terms prior to graduation, however, it dawned on me that I may have made a mistake; teaching was not the right choice. I denied myself the chance to stop and change direction. After all, I had already put in more than a year and taken out financial aid. I was not about to quit even if it turned out this was not my life's purpose. It was during this second educational crisis that I actively searched for God, Buddha, anything. Initially, I treated it as a crisis of conscience, thinking that restoring spiritual grounding in my life would provide calm for my emotional, educational, and financial storms. Having resigned myself to finishing the program, I abandoned my search for "God" and returned to regular therapy to manage my depression. Soon after graduation, I landed my first teaching job.

In the middle of my first year teaching, I was, once again, having a difficult time. A friend had suggested I take classes in massage therapy so that I could do something fun during summers off. At first, it served as a diversion. Adding classes to my teaching workload actually eased some of the stress I felt. It was a good sign. I was enjoying learning massage and every week felt excited to learn more. I did not realize that dabbling in this new skill would be the beginning of an entirely new direction in life.

Months after I stopped looking for a spiritual connection, spirituality found me. By the time the teaching year ended, massage therapy had already started changing my life by changing my outlook. I learned to trust my gut (Third Eye) when I helped clients find physical, and then emotional, relief from their pain. The most successful way I found to approach anyone's pain, whether it was new to them or they had felt it for 20 years, was to find a moment where my mind was not wandering and allow my gut feeling to come through. Soon, the sensation shifted to something even deeper, more profound. I was finally feeling connected to the Divine deep inside me (Crown). This led, in turn, to being able to tap into it so that I could connect with others, guiding them toward healing. Though the work was strenuous and challenging, I did not find it difficult. It was so natural, in fact, that there was hardly a learning curve. It felt like the kind of work I was meant to do.

As I got used to this new, profound connection I had with clients, I also found I was driven to get more done, to work harder. I had not felt so energized or motivated by any other work I had ever done. Working with clients and helping them find pain relief was empowering (Solar Plexus). When I wondered how to help them transition from pain relief to prevention, I trusted my intuition (Third Eye). The better my clients felt, the more content I was that I had made the right career choice (Heart). At 30 years old, I was discovering my purpose.

Spirituality first found me in massage school, then in Reiki training, then in the surfacing memories. Those memories were an open door. Treasure was on the other side, though it came with deep responsibility. Sometime between college and graduate school, I had promised "God" that if I was given a chance at a better life, I would dedicate my future to helping others. That was a promise I was willing to keep.

The thing that picked me up physically, emotionally, and spiritually, was massage school. By learning how to help others heal, I learned how to open my heart to the miracle of the human body, the blessing of the human experience. I learned about the transformative quality of touch. It was during training in massage therapy that my Crown Chakrum connected me to the energy of the Absolute.

Massage work was calming to me. The desperation I once felt was fading and the depression was easing. Massage and energy training complemented each other. I learned that every one of my physical pains had a reason for being there and there were also techniques to soothe and release them. I learned that my physical body was worthy of being cared for. That led me to the acceptance that my emotional and mental self was also worthy of love. Break/Through.

Showing love in a way that immediately gives it back is miraculous. The same love comes from children and animals. Massage work can heal both of these populations just as it heals me and you. Learning massage led me to learning about energy. Learning about energy led me to learning about quantum physics. From there I met a shamanic counselor and learned how deeply and completely we are all connected.

The Creator found me through each person I massaged, each person whose energy I worked with. The Creator found me though stories of abuse and survival that each client shared with me when they trusted my work. The Creator found me through nature – signs given to me by the seasons, by animals, birds, even insects. All of these parts of the universe exist in the same energy that you and I do. Learning about the Chakra System showed me how to understand the world around me, the world I move through every day.

As each of my lower Chakras went through the healing process, the effect was felt in every other Chakrum. Those Chakras that had not yet experienced active development were also reaping the benefits of increased, healthy energy flow. Today, my energy body is not as preoccupied with imbalances in my lower Chakras. Because of this, in my mid-thirties I have been able to experience a degree of spiritual awakening well before my Crown Chakrum is due to enter its own active development.

I do not regularly attend church to worship anymore because I do not feel the Creator's energy there. My tithing is through my healing work, through writing, and through the risk I take talking about survival and healing so that others can find strength to do the same. The energy of the Creator is present in every moment that I live out my purpose. For now, my purpose is to be a healer through writing, massage, and energy work. My purpose is to tell you my story and inspire you to consider your own.

10

Survival Mode:
Living with an Imbalanced Energy Body

Survival mode, in the context of the energy body, attends to the need for emotional protection and security after being harmed. Harm comes in a myriad of forms, ranging from verbal threat or intimidation to physical contact. If you have been harmed in this way at any point in your life, this need for protection is constant until you find shelter that provides the protection you need so that you can rest and recover. For some, this place is not physical. For some, this place is only available in their mind.

Survival mode is maintained by energy imbalances and their emotional and behavioral manifestations. While learning how to survive is a mechanism specific to the Root Chakrum, when you're in survival mode, all of your Chakras work together to keep your energy body functional day in and day out.

We are trained by other people's responses to us as we live our lives. As infants, before we learn to speak, we are sponges. We pick up tones, verbal and body language, and begin understanding that there is a difference between happy, sad, and angry. When we act a certain way, we get a response. When we act the opposite way, we get another response.

I entered survival mode at age two when I was no longer able to trust those closest to me. While memory of this and subsequent incidents of abuse were immediately repressed to insure my emotional survival, my energy body filed those traumatic experiences for safe keeping. Energy imbalances caused by those incidents were later acted out through my emotions and behaviors. With each incident of abuse, I learned that hiding my physical self or being as well behaved as possible would maintain my safety. Being well-behaved meant being quiet, being invisible. Staying safe meant I was buying time until life changed and I could be myself again.

During the years I was abused, each perpetrator responded to me when I was simply acting like a kid – laughing and giggling. They noticed me because I was being myself. They isolated and abused me.

Those experiences confirmed a lesson I learned early on. Being in survival mode meant it was not safe for me to be myself.

Many years later, I found I was journaling more heavily. I was already feeling and writing about the emotions I felt as I remembered more of my childhood. In addition, however, something profound was happening. I was feeling my original responses to abuse; the response I had as a child at the time the traumas occurred. When something terrorized me as a child, the details of the incident and my emotional reaction were both stored by my energy body. When a memory of abuse surfaced, the emotions I felt at the time also surfaced. As my energy body released those emotions, I felt them very strongly, perhaps just as strongly as I had felt them originally, decades earlier. As an adult, I was experiencing them as if they were brand new – raw and all-consuming. Though remembering that I was abused meant I could leave survival mode, progress and change were slow. In the meantime, additional memories only surfaced occasionally. Nearly everything they did they were accompanied by similar, palpable emotional responses.

At the moment of abuse, many children will feel a wave of fear or terror. Fight or flight kicks in, sending them straight into survival mode. It is the only safe place to be. If an adult is present and addresses the child's change in behavior, empathetic to their experience and emotions, there is a good chance for resolution and the child will not feel compelled to remain in survival mode. Even in the safest environment, where children are free to test boundaries and are gently disciplined, the ability to survive exists in their cellular structure just as it has since the beginning of time.

Learning to live in survival mode is easy. People tell you how to do it, demonstrate how it is done, and reward you when you mimic them. Every one of us has lived in survival mode. Fight or flight, that hair trigger decision to stand your ground or run away, is part of survival mode. It is part of human development, through childhood and adolescence, in every part of the world.

My experience is from life as a White female of European descent, raised in an upper-middle class White household. I grew up in the Midwestern United States. My version of survival mode will be different when compared to an African woman my age who has survived similar abuse, but who lives in the Democratic Republic of Congo. While the traumatic experiences are similar, soon family and culture will influence her particular version of survival mode. Despite how different her life experience is from mine, the impact of the original trauma on our energy bodies will be similar.

Energy flows through the body the same way, no matter your skin color, ethnic background, or cultural heritage. The way imbalances manifest, however, will look different because they are influenced by specific ethnic and cultural influences. Despite the differences between your human experience and mine, the truth is that in the end, energetic imbalances from unresolved traumas are going manifest first through our emotions, then behaviorally, and ultimately, in our physical health.

Though survival mode looks different from one person to the next, lessons about how to survive come from sources common to the human experience. We are taught how to survive by people we encounter and events we experience. Sometimes, even those that feel random and inconsequential can leave their mark. Though most of my childhood memories are hidden, one of the few that has always been available to me is from the fourth grade. Hormonal development was underway. Some of the girls' bodies had begun to change, though mine showed little sign of it. The boys in class were noticing those girls and the girls were enjoying the attention. I was hanging out with a girlfriend on the playground. Her body had been developing most rapidly of all of us. A boy from our class approached us and engaged us in conversation. He was about to teach me another way to survive.

The topic he chose was a comparison of our physical bodies. He informed us that my body was straight up and down, gesturing with hands parallel to each other, as though describing a two-by-four. His voice was flat and lacked enthusiasm. When he started describing my friend, however, his tone pepped up as he described her curves, using those same hands to gesture the outline of an hourglass. The next thing he did was turn his body toward her, cutting me off, and continued showing her attention as he changed the subject. In that moment, in the fourth grade, he put a value judgment on my physical body. I learned that by looking plain and hiding my femininity, I would be ignored. He gave me a lesson in survival.

At the time, I was already living in survival mode. If boys had noticed me the way they noticed the other girls, I probably would have been in state of panic. That boy gave me a tool that was going to be useful soon enough. Hormonally, my development eventually caught up with my friend. As my own curves developed, I learned to hide them with baggy clothes and, later, by gaining weight. I also learned that acting shy caused a lot of people to ignore me. Over time, I hid my physical body along with my personality. During my pre-teenage years, before I began making art, this behavior evolved into the desire to hide my personality and stop expressing myself, altogether. The only way to keep surviving was to hide as much of my self as I could.

I was not aware that I was in survival mode until that first memory of abuse surfaced, more than twenty years after the scene on the playground. In the moments that followed that memory, there in the dark of my bedroom, I was 31 years old and realizing that I was no longer in survival mode. I could be done with the life I had lived and that I could start living a new one. Honestly, before that moment, I did not know I had a choice. It was a new concept, the idea of living a life of my own design. It was time for me to refocus my energy; it was time to start putting myself first. I was not sure I knew how to do such a thing.

I was suddenly aware of how I was actually living. I had not realized just how many decisions I made with the intention of pleasing the elders in my life. This behavior had roots in pleasing those who abused me. Then, it occurred to me that I was also trying very hard to please my family, friends, and coworkers. I was seeking approval entirely from external sources, and once received, I translated this external reinforcement into judgments about my self-worth. If I did not receive outside approval, I felt judged and worthless.

Unaware of this survival pattern, I had replicated the cycle of self-judgment almost daily. Though it did not serve me, it was a comfortable pattern because it was predictable and controllable. I was unaware that I was doing this for nearly 20 years, or the entire time that my abuse memories were repressed. This pattern of seeking external approval felt like a yo-yo, traveling up (approval) and down (disapproval) at varying speeds. I always placed my self-worth in the hands of others.

My pattern was based on pleasing other people so that they looked upon me favorably. Each of my abusers trained me to act this way. At the same time, well-meaning, loving individuals were teaching me the same lessons. Those who loved me just used different techniques. The message was clear because I received it in so many contexts. Abusers taught me that being silent and letting them do what they wanted would please them. Pleasing them meant the pain would not last that long. Others, with loving intentions, regularly rewarded me for being such a well-behaved girl. I was happy if they were happy with me. Because of the loving intentions and rewards for being so well behaved, at the time I do not remember feeling emotionally stifled or constrained. Of course, these lessons started so early in my life that I was unaware of alternatives.

In hindsight, however, I do see signs of this in my behavior. In the fifth grade, in particular, I remember feeling and acting painfully shy. At the time, our family had moved to another state. I dismissed the feeling of shyness as a normal reaction to being the new kid in school. The feeling persisted and I accepted it as part of my personality. Having lived with it well into my 20's, I never thought to question it.

Once these abuse memories began to surface, I realized how hard I was working to please others. It dawned on me that I was tired. My energy, imbalanced as it was, was extended to others with none reserved for myself. The night that first abuse memory surfaced, my energy body initiated an overhaul process. Everything was going to change and those changes had to draw on the existing resources. Though I was willing to make changes, my energy body was so imbalanced that each move was a baby step, often accompanied by panic.

I did not want to let anyone down, or make anyone angry by putting myself first. Long ago I learned that doing such a thing was considered selfish. Such self-judgment was deeply rooted in abuse. By ignoring my own needs and, instead, pleasing others to the extent that I was physically drained, I was an active participant in my own cycle of abuse.

This new journey, a mission to heal and restore my energy and redirect it toward my own life, forced me to redefine what was selfish and unselfish. I had to change my perception. I found that when I thought about my own needs first, I ended up feeling better. This happened more and more often because I noticed that nothing bad happened to me as a consequence of mentally shifting my priorities. While I did not act on these thoughts right away, it was the practice I needed in the safety of my own mind. I had begun retraining myself.

Coupled with the epiphany about living to please others, I realized that my physical body had also suffered as a result of giving my energy away. The more journaling I did, the more aware I was of how I felt, physically. My fatigue was caused, in large part, by this energy drain. The mild depression I had lived with was also directly related to the energy drain and the fatigue. All of it was rooted in my imbalanced energy body.

Though my work as a massage therapist was energizing me, little progress was made because I was still giving away most of it. The abuse memories gave me new insight: I was not only living in survival mode, I was maintaining the lesson I learned each time I was abused. I learned that I was worthless, less than human. Anything I did to pursue my own happiness was done at my own risk. Therefore, I did very little to make myself happy. While pursuing massage therapy was a risk because of how happy it made me, it felt safe because my original intention was to work only occasionally, seeing clients during summers off from teaching.

After a year of teaching, however, I was drained and more depressed. At this point in my life, I had hit bottom emotionally and been put on an anti-depressant. I felt like I had run out of options. I decided it would be worth the risk to pursue massage therapy because I noticed that practicing it was restoring some of my energy. Desperation made the risk worthwhile.

Survival mode, for all of us, is meant to safely deliver us to an age of maturity and independent thought. When I decided to stop surviving and start living, I knew I had to take it one step at a time. In the days and months after that first memory surfaced, details of my past behaviors and choices crossed my mind one at a time. I was starting to understand that all of my physical and emotional pain was caused by my own behavior. In my recovery, this has been the most difficult thing to accept. Knowing about the energy body has made it all a bit easier to handle.

I had a mountain to scale. It was made of increasing debt, weight gain, self-abusing behaviors and self-destructive patterns. I had no choice but to admit that I created most of it in my 20's. The only reason I previously felt these behaviors were not my fault was because I was not conscious or aware of why I was behaving that way, not to mention that I had a choice in the matter. Back then, I felt worthless and depressed most of the time. Surfacing memories of trauma proved that all my self-destructive behaviors in adulthood had deep roots in childhood abuse.

Two separate truths existed in my life as I entered healing. The first truth was that I was sexually abused as a child. Being repeatedly victimized taught me to believe that my physical body and my personality lacked value; I was treated as less than human. The second truth was that the only way to change the direction of my life, having survived long enough to find safety, was to do it myself. Before I learned this, I had good intentions but always second-guessed myself. Every time, self-doubt sabotaged any success I might have had. The moment I accepted both truths was the moment I knew I could do it. The invisible oppressor, victimization, had been yanked out of the shadows and identified. It was time to be empowered.

Once I accepted those truths, I had to take responsibility for my emotions and behaviors as an adult. The next step was to realize that I was taught these behaviors. Healing began once I accepted responsibility for the state my life was in.

Your parents, teachers, friends, guardians, mentors, and others each played a role in your emotional and behavioral development. You learned which emotions were judged as appropriate, as well as which to be ashamed of and stifle. There were two methods used to teach you how to behave in childhood. The first was what your parent, teacher, etc. considered to be right and wrong based on what they had learned and/or what society deemed acceptable or unacceptable. The second happened when they were not actively teaching. In those moments, you were watching them, taking mental notes, learning how to please them even more.

The lessons you were taught by your elders worked for the patterns in their lives. Those lessons served an important purpose. They taught you how to survive in the world until you found your own footing. It is rare to recognize the moment when survival mode shifts and becomes a form of settling for less than what you are capable of achieving. It is subtle and many of us do not recognize it has happened until years later, when we are unfulfilled by our relationships and jobs, and our vision of the future is no longer a source of inspiration.

If, as a child, you learned to behave a certain way but that behavior no longer feeds your heart and soul, it is time to accept that you can do something about it. This is not to suggest that you should be ungrateful for lessons learned. On the contrary, all of what you were taught has led you to this moment. Offering up gratitude is a perfect gesture to mark the moment that you open your Crown Chakrum to inspiration and your Heart Chakrum to new possibilities.

When you accept responsibility for your current emotional and physical pain, you also accept responsibility for the love, joy and peace in your life. It is time to build on that positive energy, even if its glow is barely detectable in the shadow of overwhelming odds.

11

My Survival Mode: Behavioral Obesity

As far back as I can remember I was obsessed with my body image. Before that first abuse memory surfaced, I blamed my low self-esteem on being fat. Though I had gained and lost over the years, having maxed out at 251 pounds, I spent the better part of my 20s being fifty pounds overweight.

Before I knew about the energy body, I regularly minimized or dismissed my weight issues. In much the same way that I thought other parts of my life would never change, I also believed that I was destined to be more or less obese. It was just part of who I was, like all of my other dysfunctional emotions and behaviors. Once I learned about energy, however, I realized that *all of my bingeing was caused by imbalances in my energy body.* Most of my eating was emotional and was caused by those energy imbalances. Once I was aware of my energy body, everything changed

Your energy body not only stores memories and emotions in your muscles, joints, and cells…but also in your fat tissue.

When someone loses a significant amount of weight, it is common to say they have lost 'a whole person'. It made me wonder who or what was in that 'person' they lost. If you have lost weight in the past and eventually gained some of it back, your energy body was being set up for a new life as a thin person but had not released energy from your old life yet. There was unfinished, unresolved business in those fat cells and until it is resolved, that energy will keep creeping back. If it does not come back through weight gain it may manifest in other ways. Without resolving and releasing that old energy, the fat cells eventually need to be fed again.

Once I learned how trauma affected my energy body I saw the domino affect that followed. I was able to see more clearly how I maintained my own version of survival mode. My intention was to address each of my imbalanced Chakras, one at a time. I wanted to study how my emotions and behaviors related to the imbalances in my energy body. I was going to lift up each stone and study every detail of what lay underneath. Though it was a lot of work, I was ready.

In the darkness of that night in March when my first abuse memory surfaced I knew, somehow, that I was being given a gift. I sensed that if I could find a connection between my trauma, my energy body, and my dysfunctional behaviors, I could turn my life around. If I found the key to all of that, I could also help others to do the same.

As I moved through each Chakrum, one thing became clear. All of the imbalances in my energy body had manifested as a single behavior. This behavior went unresolved long enough that the imbalances then manifested, physically, in the most visible way: obesity.

My energy body was fertile ground for development of a destructive behavior, a behavioral vice. I was a food addict. Specific ingredients were needed depending on my emotional state. The food I required for energy and drive differed from the food I required for comfort. My needs also varied depending on how I felt on a particular day. Food played a variety of roles, including satisfying my need for love or companionship.

Once more memories of abuse began to surface I saw that my excess weight was a physical manifestation of everything I had done to survive. Studying each Chakrum, I saw how many of my unresolved energy imbalances had manifested as binge eating. When I thought about the times I binged, I realized I could remembered specific events when I felt anxious, sad, ashamed, or the like. Every one of those events had been followed up by eating something. My food addiction was maintained in a variety of ways. I ate when I needed to escape, hide, be comforted, be distracted, feel loved, or be myself without being judged.

Behavioral Obesity: Chakrum by Chakrum

Imbalances in my *Root Chakrum* created feelings of insecurity. Early on, I was shown that I could not trust others to make me feel safe. Just as other eating disorders have nothing to do with food and everything to do with control, binge eating was a way to restore my own sense of security. It was the one thing I knew would work when the rest of my life felt out of my control. I knew what happened when I ate in response to my emotions. I felt calmer and more in control of my surroundings. That was the goal. While I do not remember if I learned to eat for comfort from watching someone else or if I discovered it for myself, it was the one activity that guaranteed I would feel better about everything after I did it.

One of the results of regular bingeing to restore stability and security was steady weight gain. Every time I noticed that my clothes were getting tighter, I felt shame for continuing to binge, and felt dread about getting fatter. The truth was, I was abusing myself with food and deep down I knew it.

While my *Sacral Chakrum* was actively developing I was repeatedly traumatized. The development of my energy body was stunted. Emotionally, the erratic energy flow in my Sacral Chakrum caused me to feel stuck as I gained weight, unable to change my actions. I felt unable to change because deep down I did not actually believe I deserved to be thin and healthy. If I gained weight I would become invisible and my shame, dread and sense of failure would grow. If I lost weight, I would receive more attention, which frightened me. I was stuck. In my teens, I learned that heavier women were considered less attractive and thus received less attention. Subconsciously, this supported what I learned from the boy in 4th grade. I knew that the easiest way to hide, beyond wearing oversized clothing, was to gain weight.

By bingeing, I remained emotionally stuck. Unable to change my circumstances, I regularly felt inadequate, in despair about losing weight. All of those imbalances existed in my Sacral Chakrum and the only way to comfort myself and find emotional relief was to eat. The energy imbalance in this Chakrum sent messages of shame, embarrassment, and self-loathing to my heart and mind. This led me back to bingeing, causing more of the same emotions to be added to the pile. As long as the imbalance existed in my energy body and I was not addressing it, the emotions and behaviors continued without interruption. Until I learned about the energy body, I did not know it could stop this cycle. I honestly believed this behavior was just part of who I was. The weight kept piling on.

Though bingeing temporarily restored a sense of control, tremendous shame and embarrassment always returned in the hours and days following a session of binge eating. Paradoxically, while these emotions were uncomfortable to feel, they were familiar to me and were predictable results of my actions. Despite all evidence to the contrary, I believed I was in control.

When I ate, I did not taste what I was eating and often noticed that I was barely breathing as I put more food in my mouth. Bread was my favorite though I rarely tasted more than the first bite. I regularly got the hiccups while eating it because I was eating

149

anxiously, racing for comfort, and was holding my breath. *For me, eating was never about the food.* Even when I had sessions with the nutritionist and was learning to respect food, I still did not respect my body and, when I stopped working with her, I stopped keeping track of my food intake and returned to my old eating habits.

Every time I lived outside my means and charged more to my credit card, I followed it up with food. Before long, I could not afford to buy food without using credit, so the two vices became one. Rather than look for a job that paid a higher salary, I believed that I deserved to suffer financially and, therefore, emotionally. I did not know the source of that feeling, only that it felt true, depressing as it was.

I had such deep despair about my future (Sacral energy) and felt so out of control of my eating (Root energy), that I became overwhelmed. Though I ate to be in control, being around food actually made me feel out of control. As a result, I ate to regain the upper hand. It was the only thing in my life that I could successfully, repeatedly turn the tables on.

Imbalances in my *Solar Plexus* meant that while I was eating to maintain control of part of my life, I was actually left feeling powerless. At the time, though I felt in control of my own safety by keeping my body fat, unattractive, and unapproachable, I knew I was really only burying myself under all that weight. I felt unable to change even if I wanted to.

The development of my Solar Plexus supported my need to be in control of everything in my world. At the time that this Chakrum was developing, the energy flowing through it was being channeled into anger and rage rather than personal power, independence, and joy.

At the time that my Solar Plexus was developing, I had been abusing food for many years and was slowly gaining weight. It was only happening slowly because those were the years I was running long distance on the cross-country team. The feeling of independence, freedom, and accomplishment I felt while running were, for the time being, balancing out my usual anger, fear, and insecurity. The healthy bits of my Solar Plexus energy were giving me hints about what I was capable of and what I deserved.

When I was a long distance runner, I was within thirty pounds of a healthy weight. Running enabled me to feel strong and free, and for the few short months that I trained I was reminded that I could kick this weight thing if I wanted to. That reminder would usually cross my mind as the season ended. I could have continued to run but came up with many excuses not to. The only routes I knew were near school, I did not want to do it alone, and I was too afraid of being seen running in my own neighborhood. Behaviorally, my Solar Plexus did not have enough power to shift the balance of my energy body in a positive direction.

I learned many things about fat when I was growing up. In addition to the Root Chakrum insecurity and the shame and self-judgment from my Sacral Chakrum, my Solar Plexus contributed something invisible in my journey to obesity. It took many more years to admit, but I had developed a prejudice against other overweight people. My prejudice was rooted in my own sense of powerlessness. The prejudice was entirely fear-based, as prejudices commonly are.

At the time I was gaining weight, judging others was only way I knew to lift the pressure off myself. I could judge other obese people and mentally direct my anger toward them. It was easy to do because it all happened in the safety of my own mind. Judging them instantly relieved me. When I decided they were obviously more out of control than I was my ego bounced back a bit.

It was easy to find someone overweight to look at and pass judgment on. Though I restricted judgments to my own mind, in those moments I had the chance to leave my dread behind and point the imaginary finger at someone else. I found that silently judging obese people temporarily helped me feel much better about myself. Every opportunity came to an abrupt end when I realized they reminded me of *me*. Time passed, I started feeling horrible about myself, and, conveniently forgetting just how the exercise always ended, did it again. This behavior did not end until after the abuse memories began surfacing.

When children are abused, they are given a clear message that they are not worthy of love, affection, or protection. Though all of my abuse was sustained before my *Heart Chakrum* actively developed, the energy flowing through that part of my energy body had already been deeply affected. The imbalance in my Heart energy manifested, emotionally, as a lifelong need to find someone who would be willing to love me despite how worthless I was. Unfulfilling relationships led to loneliness and emptiness. These emotions, which I felt more and more regularly, drove me to use food as distraction.

Deep down I was starting to sense that I was using food in a destructive manner. Being my only source of stability, however, I realized I needed to change my perception and change it fast. I decided that I felt better considering food as a source of love, allowing myself to be comforted by the fact that it was always there. It was a nonjudgmental, predictable companion. At the time, I did not care that I was simply changing the label without changing the behavior. Once memories of abuse began to surface, however, everything changed.

By addressing emotions related to my imbalanced Sacral Chakrum, I started changing my behavior. Over time, I reversed my debt pattern and spending habits. I started doing something I previously considered impossible; living within my financial means. I was only able to do this after I started my healing process because I could finally see, clearly, that the value I put on my own life had nothing to do with my income. My life was devalued by those who abused me long before I had the chance to learn how important I actually was. Behaviorally, I kept myself devalued with low paying jobs and weight gain.

When I got used to living within my means, a new food-related behavior surfaced. It manifested when I admitted that I could not even regularly afford to buy groceries. I asked for help from human services and was given food from a local food bank. I also started using food stamps. Days passed and I ate the food I had received. As

I noticed it dwindle, I felt the old anxiety growing. As I approached the day I could go back and get another box, I felt guilty for still needing assistance. It was as if I thought I could have turned my economic picture around in one month if I had only tried harder.

The next thing I noticed was that I felt possessive about the food that I had not eaten yet. Friends came over and wanted to make dinner, combining their food and mine. I panicked. While I did not want to turn down the chance to share dinner with friends, I was already so ashamed about the source of my food that sharing it with friends made everything worse. The food was in the cupboard as though I bought it myself, but I knew the truth and was deeply afraid of being judged. I realized that I was coveting my food, afraid that I would starve once it was gone.

With friends in the kitchen using my food, I could not think straight. Imbalances in my Heart Chakrum were manifesting as obsession (coveting the food), and feeling trapped (forced into sharing) and claustrophobic. Part of the healing that came out of this experience happened when I returned to the food bank a few days later. I had been able to forgive myself for feeling possessive about my food. I allowed myself to embrace, and then be grateful for, the additional support. In the context of my behavioral obesity, I was clearing a hurdle. Years after seeing that nutritionist, I was forced to start seeing food as fuel once again. I had to work on healing my binge behavior because it was obvious that I could no longer financially afford it. I had to accept that I could no longer emotionally afford it, either. Using food as a vice was no longer doing me any good and had to be yanked out of the darkness.

While my Heart energy was imbalanced and partially contributed to my behavioral obesity, my *Throat Chakrum* had sustained some of the most significant damage and pushed me toward food most often. The energy imbalance in my Throat manifested in two ways, guaranteeing steady weight gain. Early on, I learned that if something felt wrong and I spoke up, I would get hurt. The first major lesson was to distract myself so that I would keep quiet. If a situation made me feel uneasy, out of control, insecure, ashamed, angry, or trapped, I learned that eating would immediately comfort me by distracting me.

The second lesson developed as an oral fixation. When I was abused as a three year-old, I was orally raped. This incident taught me to always be putting something in my mouth. It was comforting, it calmed me, and somewhere deep down I was reminded of what a good girl I was for doing what I was told. Needing to hide in a fatter body and finding comfort in food, oral fixation was the perfect behavioral companion.

With the need for food clouding all of my lower Chakras, the energy flowing through my *Third Eye* and *Crown* was forced to compensate to balance my energy body and were not available to offer the insight and guidance they were designed to provide. Imbalances in my Third Eye manifested as anxiety about the future and an inability to stop analyzing what was wrong with me. The only way I was able to shut off either of those noises was by eating.

Another manifestation of imbalance in my Third Eye was to set too high of standards for myself and those around me. This meant that I was regularly disappointed. In my 20's I admitted to someone that being disappointed made me feel so terrible that it was the worst thing I thought I was capable of feeling. Every time that I was disappointed by someone, I felt abandoned. When they did not meet my expectations, it meant they did not value me as a person. That was my signal to reach for food. It was my comfort and never, ever disappointed me.

157

Imbalance in my Crown Chakrum led to mild depression and lethargy. Additionally, my imbalanced Crown manifested in an inability to focus on learning and retaining information. Throughout my education, I had the built-in belief that I was stupid. In high school, I used my bad memory as my excuse for lower scores in certain subjects. The truth was I was simply not interested in much of what they taught in school. I had no problem getting A's in the subjects I felt passionate about. The imbalance created by disinterest and passion resulted in an average showing all the way through graduate school. Beneath it all I struggled to learn what I was not interested in, which made me feel stupid, at the same time that I considered any academic success a fluke.

As it turns out, while my surfacing memories do not include details like dialogue, it is possible that I was told I was stupid during the times I was abused. Regardless, I know that I felt, deeply, that I must have been stupid to have been abused in the first place, not to mention so many other times afterward. Feeling stupid often drove me right back to binge eating for comfort.

Having a bad memory meant there was another thing about me that was inherent, dysfunctional and unchangeable. Combine those elements and mix in a crisis of faith, believing that "God" abandoned me early on, and it will come as no surprise that I turned back to the predictable, safe embrace of food.

Fat: The Story of my Life

In my family, obesity is not genetic. Hypothyroidism may be, though I am the only living family member with a diagnosis and, before me, it skipped two generations. As a child and adolescent, I dieted frequently to lose ten or twenty pounds because I regularly felt fat. The earliest documented attempt at "another diet" was in a family log book and I was 12 years old. Years later, at age 17, I went on a pre-packaged food diet and lost 30 pounds. It came off easily because I was running on that Cross Country team at the time.

Of course, when the season ended, so did my running. That just happened to coincide with my weight hitting a plateau. At least that is what the people at the diet office called it. Truth be told, a boy in my high school class had noticed my weight loss and made a comment…and I went home and promptly began snacking more heavily. The comment had sent my energy body into a panic, though as far as I knew I was just bored with the diet and wanted to eat normal food again.

For me, eating normally meant I started snacking after school and ate until dinner. Most of that was hidden from my parents because I was ashamed of doing it. It was lonely eating, bored eating, behavioral eating. In the case of the boy at school noticing me, it was also eating out of fear.

While I may have gained back about ten pounds by snacking, I was still twenty pounds thinner than when I started that diet. Soon, I graduated and moved to college. To maintain my weight loss, I went running at the track every day and did some light weight training. After a couple weeks I decided I felt confident enough to weigh myself. I was heavier than I expected to be considering that, in addition to my workouts, I had been carefully avoiding most of my bingeing behavior. That is when I decided to weigh myself more regularly. Without fail, I was gaining about pound a week. Though I had done everything right and should have been losing weight, I felt the familiar pangs of shame and self-loathing because I must have done *something* wrong.

Around this time, an anomaly was found in how my thyroid gland was functioning. A letter was sent to me at home suggesting I come in for additional tests. Though the initial blood test was performed before I left for college, the follow up was not done until I returned, nine months later. By that time, I had re-gained all the weight I lost on that pre-packaged diet plus another twenty pounds. The blood test confirmed the problem. I was put on medication to regulate my sluggish thyroid. While this meant I could start losing weight if I wanted to, I was too angry and resentful to even try.

For years I was angry at the doctor for not stressing more urgent action, angry at myself for not speaking up when I saw my weight skyrocketing, and, most of all, angry at my body for ceasing production of thyroid hormones. The one method I had regularly used for comfort was now used to punish.

If I wanted to, I could have returned to healthy eating and exercise and it was guaranteed to work. My doctor, the same one who sent the letter home, promised me that. I did not follow his advice and, instead, even gained some more weight just to spite him. While I knew I was behaving irrationally, I was not done being angry.

Before I knew it, I was blaming myself for letting six years pass before I considered doing anything about it. I was exhausted from being so angry. Finally, I was ready to change some things. Coincidentally, when I was ready to act I happened to be working at a job with excellent benefits. One of the employees had lost a significant amount of weight by working with a nutritionist who was covered by insurance.

At 251 pounds, I made an appointment and started weekly sessions. After a few weeks of walking to work out (because it hurt too much to run), I lost enough weight to start a combination of running and walking. The nutritionist taught me how to keep a food diary. While she did not require that I write down my feelings along with what I ate, she always asked me how I felt about the food I had documented.

I was consistently applauded for what I enjoyed and savored. She also regularly scolded my behavior when I admitted to eating for comfort. Eating that way meant I was not paying attention to what I put in my mouth. Her point was *why eat if I am not going to enjoy every last morsel*?

Years later, I realized that when food is made with love and then eaten with love, that much more love enters my energy body. If food is rushed through, *inhaled*, or worse yet, eaten while angry or resentful, my energy body is likewise affected. It is possible that food is even metabolized differently when consumed while feeling joy, gratitude, appreciation, and other positive emotions. In addition, when I did not give my food the attention it needed to metabolize well, I was not respecting it…and that really meant I was not respecting myself. As long as I disrespected myself, I could not permanently lose weight. All of this happened years before my abuse memories surfaced. That meant that, while I would try to lose weight time and again, I was not yet aware of the root cause of my binge behavior. Without knowing why, I was regularly disrespecting myself by using food to answer all of my emotional needs. Because of this, it felt impossible to lose more than a handful of pounds and keep them off.

In the end, working with the nutritionist helped me lose nearly 90 pounds. I thought I should have been ecstatic, but instead…something seemed strange to me. I had lost that much weight, I fit into smaller sized clothing, the number on the scale proved it, my favorite jeans that I had not been able to wear for two years were baggy, I could wear the Irish sweater that used to make me feel fat because it hugged my waist, my stomach was nearly flat, I saw a thin reflection in the windows I ran by during daily workouts…and something seemed strange. At the same time that I was in shock at the little number on the scale and my reflection in the mirror, deep down nothing had changed.

I still felt obese. Though I weighed 160, I felt no different than when I was 251 pounds. On the surface I could tell things were different. Friends acted more excited to see me, strangers who used to ignore me now made eye contact and even greeted me, and my old clothes were so loose I could not wear them anymore. In the back of my mind, however, was a convincing voice telling me that those clothes were just stretched out and needed to be run through the dryer. Again.

I felt safe when I was 251 pounds. No one noticed me. Even in public, I had been invisible. I was protected, my survival guaranteed. Seeing my thin image in the mirror, however, or feeling my once tight clothes hanging on my frame, was enough to send my energy body into a panic. At the time, all I knew was that I was really uncomfortable because the fat clothes that used to fit did not fit well anymore. They had been comforting to me but, suddenly, I could not hide in them.

The day I weighed in at 160 pounds, my nutritionist took out a rubber model the size of a brick, labeled "1 lb", and handed it to me.

As I was processing the fact that I had lost 90 of those, she told me things had to change with my care. For months, she had talked to me about my feelings when I ate certain things. There was only one thing in common between the chocolate on Monday, the half-pizza on Thursday, and the vegetables, rice and beans on Sunday. Every one of those meals provided comfort and filled a void unrelated to hunger. She told me that my needs could no longer be met by her specific training as a nutritionist. It was time, she said, to see a therapist.

The part of my weight loss that addressed food was taken care of. The rest of it was about something else. I felt betrayed and abandoned but kept quiet because I also felt stupid for having that reaction.

I was referred to a doctor down the hall. She was a psychiatrist and was skinny and I spent all my time thinking about her bony knees. How could she identify with me? After all, I was fat. Sitting in front of her, I was 160 pounds and felt like 251. For months, she tried to help me understand how much weight I lost and feel how thin and fit I actually was. It did not work. While I felt good receiving weekly time for myself, something still did not seem right. I was as tired and depressed as I had ever been. There were no immediate answers and therapy was not helping.

If I was healthier I could have seen that this therapist was mirroring my newly trim and fit body. My perception had not been altered at all, though, so what I saw only made me feel badly about myself. I felt weird. It was my first time realizing I could not really feel my body. I sat there on her couch and was also numb, emotionally. I had no physical or emotional sense of what I had accomplished. My energy body was so imbalanced that I was incapable of feeling pride, self-love, or joy as a result of my dramatic weight loss.

Over the next few years, I left that job and its benefits behind in favor of graduate school. At the same time, I gained much of that weight back. I stopped at 70 pounds instead of gaining back all 90. In graduate school, while training for the teaching career that I already doubted, I returned to food for comfort. Food was the only consistent support system I trusted. This time the difference was that I paid attention to what I was eating, even when I binged. I disrespected food and I knew, deep down, what that meant.

In graduate school I binged because I had a feeling it was not the right place for me to be but I was too afraid to quit. Not only was I afraid that I did not know how to make my dreams a reality, I was realizing that I did not actually know what those dreams even were. My authentic self was not fat, but I had failed at being thin. My authentic self was not an office manager or secretary, but I also knew I did not feel like a teacher. When asked, I would usually say I wanted to help others and change the world. That is the answer of a child. Behaviorally, I was still functioning at that level. I was lost.

Over the next couple of years, I followed through with graduate school and became a teacher. The stress of teaching, combined with a long commute to the school, left little time to binge for comfort. In the middle of that year, I experienced my emotional rock bottom, followed, within weeks, by the beginning of massage school. I was spinning from one career to the next while maintaining a weight that was 50-60 pounds heavier than healthy.

By maintaining that weight, I proved to myself that I could hold steady. Gaining any more than that would have come too close to my heaviest. I had promised myself I would never to return to that weight and that was a promise I intended to keep. I controlled my weight by exercising occasionally and then allowing myself to eat comfort foods in order to make up for the calories burned. This was the method I used to sustain my behavioral obesity. I called my activity *controlling* my weight rather than *maintaining* it because my binge eating and exercise were inconsistent and likely to be harmful to my heart, not to mention the rest of my physical body.

Fast forward a few years. The days after that first abuse memory surfaced, when I realized I could change everything about my life, I noticed that my appetite had already shifted a bit. The more driven I was to find answers and unravel behaviors, the less I needed to binge. My perception of food as comfort began to dissolve, ever so slightly. I was surprised to find that I did not need it to be a safety net nearly as often because I had begun journaling and that was helping take the edge off in a way I never expected. The more writing I did, the more time passed between bingeing episodes.

Without trying, as I started healing my energy body, I also started losing weight. Somehow, I was curing myself of behavioral obesity, something I used to believe was a prison from which there was no escape. The more weight I lost, the more I felt like exercising. The more active I was, the more weight I lost, the more inspired I was to start respecting food again. I event started cooking and baking regularly, sharing the results with coworkers and friends. Food was losing its stigma, coming out into the open again, and returning to its proper place as sustenance and something to be celebrated. While the binge eating still existed, it had melted from being a monster larger than me, to being a tiny emotionally-driven behavior that I started sensing from miles away.

12

Everything Changes

Though it started in my teens, the older I got the more fear, and sometimes paranoia, I felt. At the time, I could not put my finger on why this was happening. While I was always afraid of dying, it felt more sinister to me. I did not know to identify it as my energy body sending me signals. Everything made more sense that night my abuse memories began to surface. In a matter of hours, two things occurred to me. Though they were two distinct ideas, in my mind they were linked. First, my once pervasive sense of fear and paranoia seemed to dissolve almost completely. Most noticeably, I was no longer afraid to die. The second was that I felt compelled to write everything down.

In my younger years, I rarely kept a diary. Though some of my friends did it, I was disinterested. Later, when journaling became trendy, I noticed that I had a negative reaction anytime I considered writing down details from my life. Though I used the excuse of having no time to spend doing it, the truth was that I thought my life was not worth documenting. The moment I remembered being abused, however, I not only had the desire to write, I felt the need to.

Writing enabled me to think more clearly almost immediately. I realized I did not have to take responsibility for what was done to me. *I could, however, accept what I saw in that moment, and take responsibility for my future.* Though I wanted everything about my life to change all at once, deep down I knew that was not about to happen. I had to start somewhere. The first step was to start writing regularly.

It was an unstructured activity from the beginning. When I decided to start, I did not have anything to write in. I felt a mixture of adrenaline and anxiety rising. Running to the store would take too much time, so instead I rummage through my art supplies, found an old sketchbook, and started there. One of the things that used to intimidate me about journaling or keeping a diary was being embarrassed about my penmanship. I did not want to ruin a pretty journal by filling its pages with my erratic style of handwriting. In this context, that old sketchbook was a perfect fit.

So many things crossed my mind that I decided to suspend all pre-conceived notions about what journaling should look like. If I needed to sketch a picture because words did not describe the experience, I did. Lines on a page became arbitrary. The more I wrote, the better I felt. Though I was not totally aware of it at the time, my energy body was releasing so much information it sometimes felt like I had uncorked myself. The flow was steady and strong. It was habit forming. I had to keep writing.

I found that if I made time every morning, to write down what was on my mind, the rest of the day I felt calmer and more clear-headed. It occurred to me that by writing, I was taking the load of what burdened my energy body and was setting it down, permanently, in my journal. *I was meeting my own emotional needs on a daily basis*. By doing that, I found that some of my old behaviors were changing.

At the end of a busy day, I was able to find calm more easily. I started forgetting my old habit of reaching for food the moment I walked in the door. The television and couch were not as enticing as they had been. Instead of eating in front of the television, I found myself cleaning, reading, or going through paperwork. I did not toss and turn before falling asleep. I started to remember my dreams. The dreams became more vivid. Soon, I noticed that I was not depressed and realized that I had actually not felt that way for months. I was surprised but not shocked. Even my emotional reactions were turning into more gentle responses. I still felt all the same emotions but the desperation that used to make them feel so dramatic was absent.

Documenting what weighed on my mind and my heart actually removed weight from my energy body. The more I wrote about my emotions and let myself feel them as they surfaced, the lighter I felt. Through writing, my weak Throat Chakrum was acting as a shovel, slowly digging up the traumas that buried all my other Chakras. I scooped up negative energy from the top of each pile and tossed it into my journal. Almost from the beginning, my Third Eye energy pitched in and added insight to help me along. By journaling regularly, I was thinking more clearly.

Some days I felt anger rise up and found that my handwriting became illegible as the pen yelled into the journal. A single written word filled the page. The next word filled the next page. While I considered slowing down, writing more carefully, I realized that the point was not always to preserve every detail of my life. *Sometimes the point of journaling was simply to let go of things that no longer served me*. These illegible scrawls were documenting things that I would never have to revisit.

Journal writing evolved into using more than a pen to document my life. Sometimes I used markers, sometimes pencils, crayons, or pastels. There were also times I had something on my mind but did not have my journal with me. Those times I gave myself permission to write on anything I could find – legal pad, printer paper, scratch paper, napkin, once even a bank receipt. When I returned home I stuffed those bits into the journal.

Part of the support I received at the rape crisis center was a lesson in a technique called non-dominant handwriting. This technique taps into a different part of the brain than is active when using your dominant hand. I am right handed, so I switched to my left and started to write. Struggling to make the shape of every letter, I saw what looked like a child's handwriting. Psychologically, I was told, this might stimulate my brain to feel or think the way I did when I first learned to write.

The first time I did this, I was quickly frustrated. It took a long time to even get comfortable with the feeling of the pen in my other hand. I decided to try making art that way, instead. The painting that came out of my left hand was beautiful, restoring my confidence. I decided to try writing again. This time, I allowed the frustration to rise and felt it pass. The third time, I wrote for a long time and found that I was documenting small details about my childhood. There were even moments when my writing voice switched and I wondered if that was what I sounded like when I was little. Whether using my dominant or non-dominant hand, using a pen, crayon, or other tool, journaling was nudging my brain into letting go.

For me, journaling was about unpacking emotional boxes, heavy with memories and experiences, boxes that had been in storage for way too long. There were treasures in there. There was also some really old stuff that needed to be disposed of. For me, writing became about letting go of everything that my energy body had held onto. All of this stuff no longer served me. Some of it had other people's names, faces, or voices in it; some of it was my own.

Letting go meant I was cleaning house. While making more space for growth and healing was a scary proposition, my intuition had made it clear: I really did not have a choice anymore. *If I was serious about changing my life, digging out the truth and finally living, I had to keep writing, keep shoveling, keep working.*

175

Growing up, I was told that the only way to truly love others was to love myself, first. In general, while I had agreed with that notion my whole life, I did not actually know how to do it until I started journaling. The more I wrote, the more I learned about myself. With insight from my Third Eye, I was able to uncover my buried Heart Chakrum. As time passed, my sense of self-loathing slowly leaked out, making room for self-love. *Writing had become a powerful tool in my healing process.*

Writing is a simple activity. I chose to write because of how accessible it was and how honest I could be. Before I knew what was happening, it changed my life. By writing on a regular basis I was able to strengthen the healthy flow of energy in each of my Chakras and address their imbalances. Sometimes weeks would pass without a journal entry because things were happening so fast I did not take time to document them. I always returned to journaling, however, because I knew it was the one tool that guaranteed I would stay on track.

Writing taught me to listen to my energy body. For example, sometimes working with clients left me drained and, occasionally, I even felt resentment toward them. The truth was, while they continued to come see me I was sometimes too tired to effectively help

176

them. The resentment was caused by my imbalanced Heart Chakrum energy. I did not want to feel that way about anyone, so I wrote about it. Admitting how I felt, the sensations eased and then lifted. My energy body had only needed me to notice that something was off-kilter so that it could let go of that energy and open my eyes to the truth. The cause of my resentment was my own sense of neglect. I was not taking sufficient care of myself. Once I stepped up my self-care regiment, things returned to normal; I felt revitalized by my work once again. Feeling empathy and compassion for people without having it drain me meant that my Heart Chakrum energy was on the mend.

Listening to my energy body taught me that many of my physical sensations were actually energy-based, as well. One day, a few years into healing, I was running and felt sudden pain in my knees and ankles. I had been running regularly for months and had not felt soreness like that in quite awhile. I panicked. My breathing became erratic.

I stopped running and tried to walk it out. Walking and stretching did not help. Panic turned into frustration and then fear. Within seconds, fear turned to anger. My Solar Plexus, that center of personal power, was imbalanced and flaring. I did not deserve to feel pain. Months before, my gut feeling was that it would be good for me to start running again. Now I felt like I was being punished for listening to it. All of the old, dramatic sensitivities were coming up at the same time. Feeling pain was unacceptable…but my angry reaction was clouding my Third Eye, my ability to think rationally. I had to calm down.

Taking a deep breath as I walked, I was reminded of how intuition always steered me in the right direction. It occurred to me to stop walking. I knew the energy body was affected by intention and focus. I had the sense that my pain was energy based because it came on so suddenly and I could not pinpoint exactly where it hurt; the sensations were moving around a bit. My gut sense was that nothing was torn or sprained. Closing my eyes, my intention was to let the aches drain from my knees and ankles into the ground.

Within a couple of moments, feeling no different physically, it occurred to me to open my eyes and start running again. I still felt the aches, but they were different. They were different because I had the added sense that they were about to disappear. I continued running, mindful of not pushing myself. A few minutes later, I realized that the pain was gone.

Writing taught me to trust my intuition and my intuition showed me how to listen to my body. Originally, I learned to listen to my intuition and my body in massage school. At the time, however, my energy was so imbalanced that I did not trust my gut in the first place. Years later, as writing cleared up the vision in my Third Eye, I found myself easily able to tap into, and trust, my sixth sense.

These days, while I still have a Western-trained medical doctor to turn to when I need her, I listen to my body first. The more I trusted myself, the healthier my ego and identity became. These are the energies of a stronger, more balanced Solar Plexus. Though I felt my anger flare the day I was running and felt the pain sensations, I was able to channel that energy into a highly efficient moment of healing.

Of course, there have been many times that I have chosen not to write because I knew something was coming that would be difficult to accept. I did not always want to remember things from my past or feel the related emotions, even though I knew that once they came up I could let them go. Sometimes I needed a break.

179

When I allowed for distraction, first thing I did was to pair food with something visual. I would either eat in front of the television or go to a coffeehouse and surf the web. Either way the itch was scratched. Hours passed, my belly was stuffed, and I remembered little of what I had done. Most importantly, I had successfully avoided some hard work. I had passed on an opportunity to break through and heal another part of my imbalanced energy body. For a couple of years after that first memory of abuse surfaced, if I gave into distraction it was really difficult to return to writing and healing afterward. It was like falling off the wagon and having to start over.

Most of what I saw around me I ended up having to label as distraction. I did this to draw boundaries for myself as I continued to heal. Difficult as it was to break away from television, movies, magazines, and internet, all I had to do was look back at my previous journal entry to remind myself of how much I had already accomplished. Falling off the wagon only meant I temporarily lost my balance. The wagon stopped the moment I fell off it. It would wait for me until I was ready to climb back on. The journey resumed the moment I started writing again.

As months passed and I filled up more journals, the less I dreaded speaking up when my voice was not being heard. Though I could not tell where it was coming from, I also felt more confident as I helped clients through difficult healing sessions. I was learning how important it was to take responsibility not only for my actions but for my words. My Throat Chakrum was getting stronger.

Over time, I noticed that I felt better for longer periods between waves of depression, regret or anxiety. When I did feel those sensations again, however, they felt much stronger than I had remembered. This was unexpected. I had assumed that when I felt better overall the intensity of such emotions would automatically fade. They did not. I realized that I had a lot of this negative energy buried in layers.

Every time I felt the next wave growing after feeling so good, I had to remind myself that it was actually the next layer ready to be released. Though I was no longer worn down by those strong emotions, I still found them very difficult to work through. There was a new lesson to learn. I had to keep reminding myself that I had a choice. I could focus on how badly I felt in that moment, holding onto the sensation, or I could take a deep breath and allow myself to feel it as though it was a breeze blowing through. I did not have to hold onto it. I was only feeling it at that moment because my energy body was ready to let it go.

The more I trusted myself to be able to handle the challenging emotions that surfaced, the happier I was. My Sacral and Heart Chakrum imbalances were being addressed. Financially, I spent these years reversing the pattern of debt I had been in and started to see the baby steps of recovery. An increasing sense of financial balance brought with it a growing sense of relief. Deep in my Sacral Chakrum, healing was in progress.

Journaling also helped me to discover another side of myself. While I knew I was a visual artist, having been trained in those summer classes and during school, I did not know that I was also a writer. It was an epiphany.

Living in survival mode required that I continually self-stifle, regularly silencing myself. The only voice I had to share with the world had been stifled, insecure, and full of self-doubt. Until the moment I remembered being abused, I had believed that my voice was not worth using, that I did not have anything worthwhile to say.

Writing showed me there was a more enlightened way of looking at my life. It guaranteed safety and allowed me the freedom to choose where, when or even *if* I was going to write. It allowed me to be myself in every way. Writing became my constant companion as I made my way back to the life that had been waiting for me all along.

Through writing, I found a deeper understanding of my energy body. Understanding my energy body meant I finally had a proper map for my healing journey. Learning about my energy body freed me from survival mode, enabling me to start searching for my life purpose. For more than twenty years, I lived in a cycle of debt, depression, and ill-health. Healing myself, one Chakrum at a time, uncovered reasons why I felt so stuck and was living such a stagnant life. Some energy imbalances can be released and healed without knowing the details. Others, however, compel me to study them because they contain profound messages that permanently change my life.

Energy is not meant to be stagnant. There will always be something to address - whether a gut feeling, an emotion, a behavior, or something physical. In this human experience, we are not meant to belabor this fact but, rather, embrace it. By acknowledging and respecting our own experiences, past and present, we become more compassionate people. By acknowledging the truth held in our energy fields, we are releasing that which bound us, that which held us back from feeling truly alive. By healing our energy fields, one Chakrum at a time, we can finally thrive.

About the Author

Katie Custer is a minister, writer, internet radio host, massage therapist, energy worker, artist, and teacher. She has a B.A. in Fine Arts (Loyola University Chicago), a Master of Science in Education and Social Policy (Northwestern University), a diploma in massage therapy (Chicago School of Massage Therapy), and has received training up to Reiki III. She is currently preparing for training as a Reiki Master Teacher.

In 2008, Katie created an alter-ego called "Chakra Girl," and works from this platform to inspire people to study their own energy fields so that they can heal and discover the deepest roots of who they are, engaging and celebrating their life's purpose. She writes a weekly column called "Ask Chakra Girl," and can be found blogging about how everything is energy at *www.chakra-girl.com*. She also hosts Chakra Girl Radio (CGR), a weekly talk show dedicated to studying the human energy body and how energy is reflected back to us in our daily lives. Chakra Girl Radio is found online at *www.blogtalkradio.com/chakra-girl*, airing live on Wednesdays,

9:00-10:30 a.m. PST, with archives available anytime. Downloadable podcasts are available at the same address.

In fall 2008, Katie began focusing on the human energy body in the context of information about energy acceleration discovered by the Mayan people, now called the Mayan Calendar. This Calendar mathematically outlines how energy has evolved in our Universe, and our planet, since the Big Bang. In this Calendar, the Mayan people documented the acceleration of creation energy through the year 2012. Each week, Chakra Girl Radio is dedicated to helping listeners make the connection between energy acceleration in the Universe (in politics, the economy, world events, natural disasters, etc) and how it stimulates their own energy body toward healing.

In January 2009, Katie established Chakra Girl Ministries. As its founder and Executive Director, her intention is to provide support and guidance to those ready to acknowledge how energy is affecting them, while helping them improve their health, their relationships, and their lives. The outreach blog for Chakra Girl Ministries is www.chakra-girl.com. Katie maintains a private practice in Oregon, USA.